The Myth of the Armed Citizen

Michael R. Weisser

in collaboration with

William A. Weisser

Volume 6: Guns in America

Published by:

TeeTee Press
Ware MA 01082

Cover design by Damonza

ISBN: 0692557768
ISBN-13: 978-0692557761

10 9 8 7 6 5 4 3 2 1

First Edition

To my best friend Leonard Savetsky and the blessed memory of Herman Smotiler

CONTENTS

CHAPTER 1

BEFORE THE MYTH

When I was 11 years old in 1955, I belonged to a shooting club sponsored by the NRA. The club met Friday afternoon following school at my brother's junior high school, which was located a few blocks from the grammar school where I was enrolled. My brother's junior high school had an honest-to-God rifle range in the basement with two or three full-length lanes, and we shot old bolt-action 22-caliber training rifles that had been used in the Army in both world wars, then given to the NRA and then given to my club and clubs all over the USA.

The biggest treat was that after practice or sometimes a match, we were allowed to take the guns home for the weekend which meant walking about a mile from the school to my home with the gun held in a little cloth sack. It wasn't hard to figure out that I was carrying a gun. And when I got it home I would clean it, play with it, fool around with it, pretend to shoot a squirrel in the backyard, and then give it to my brother to take back to his junior high at the beginning of the week.

Now you might think that I grew up in Topeka or Little Rock or some flyover smaller town in a city and state where it was not unusual to see people walking around with guns. In fact I was born and raised in Washington, DC and my brother's junior high school, which is now called MacFarland Middle School, still sits on Iowa Avenue in the Petworth neighborhood which is where my family lived from 1950 to 1956. I was born at Garfield Hospital in 1944.

This was what guns were all about when I was a kid. You could walk through a dense, urban neighborhood in the nation's capitol with a gun and nobody cared. In the same way that when I went downtown and visited the museum in the old NRA headquarters on New Hampshire Avenue I was usually the only one there. The NRA might have been located on Pennsylvania Avenue, I'm really not sure. But it was somewhere downtown, walking distance from the Mall and, like I said, I was usually the only one wandering around the exhibit hall.

That was then, this is now. If you walked down a street in DC with a gun in a cloth sack you better be filming a movie and the gun still better not be real. Two years after the D.C. District Court told the DC Police that they had to start issuing permits to let people keep unlocked guns in their home, never mind walk around with a banger in their pocket, the cops still haven't really figured out what to do. As for the NRA, if they hadn't moved to a new headquarters building out in the burbs in 1995, I guarantee you that every day there would be a couple of t-shirted Moms walking up and down in front of the building telling all and sundry that the occupants were, as my grandmother used to say, up to no good.

I don't know how much the world has changed in the last sixty years, but I can tell you that the whole question of guns in this country has changed a great deal. Sixty years ago, there was at least one gun in every other American home. In states that still had lots of farms and people living in small towns, per capita gun ownership was easily 75 percent. These numbers are essentially extrapolations from surveys that were conducted in the 1960s and 1970s but they are nonetheless correct.[1] And don't forget that until the early 70s there had been a universal military draft, which meant that just about every able-bodied male learned how to use a rifle and a pistol even if they chose not to keep a gun around when they returned to civilian life.

The latest data from the General Social Survey shows that gun ownership has now fallen to one-third of all American households, certainly far less in the northeast. In fact, with a few exceptions, the states with the highest per-capita gun ownership today are also states with small populations, which means that in the overall scheme of things they don't count for very much. The ten states where per capita gun ownership is above 50 percent total all together a bit more than 17 million residents, or 5 percent of the country's population as a whole.[2] That's not a lot of people even though on a per capita basis they each own lots of guns.

Actually, when you stop to think about it, even if only one-third of all American households contain a legal firearm, it still means that the number of Americans living in gun-owning families is somewhere north of 100 million which, in and of itself makes American gun owners the thirteenth or fourteenth largest country in the world. That's a lot of people, when all is said and done, and if we can believe the NRA's membership numbers as being somewhere around 4 million, then that's a lot of people too. Particularly when they are now fed a daily, and I mean a daily dose of news, videos, shopping opportunities and emergency letters that need to be sent to Washington to complain about all kinds of threats to their guns.

I am still a member of the NRA; in fact I'm a Life Member, which means that I gave the organization a chunk of dough some years ago and now don't have to think about renewing my membership every year. The reason I signed up had nothing to do with their stated purpose of protecting me and my guns, but rather, because of my admiration and interest in the historical articles which appear each month in the *American Rifleman* magazine which doesn't cost anything beyond my dues. The articles on the history of guns, both American and foreign, put the Smithsonian to shame, and if the NRA were ever to publish a collection of these articles as a series of books I would buy every single one (hint, hint).

I'm also a member of *Everytown* and the *Brady Campaign*, the two leading organizations on the other side of the gun debate, but I'm not really a member because they don't have memberships, they simply send out emails asking for cash. And once I give them a donation I'm on their lists forever more. What do I get from these organizations beyond more appeals for dough? Nothing. Nothing at all. Meanwhile, the NRA sends me opportunities to buy cheap medical insurance and cheap liability insurance covering my guns. I can also build a nice wine collection courtesy of their online shop, and let's not forget the clothing, the outdoor gear, the CDs on gun safety, the merchandising goes on and on.

But you know what? It works. And it works because the basic message, and it has always been the NRA message, is that if you own a gun then you share something very special and unique with everyone else who owns a gun. And just as important, or even more important, you are different from anyone and everyone who *doesn't* own a gun.

It's this sense of being different, of being special because of gun ownership, which makes the NRA such a powerful and compelling brand. There's really nothing like it in any other membership experience that I have been involved with, say, for example, the AAA or AARP. Both of those organizations offer specific member services, both of them inundate me with publications, online and printed merchandising and God knows, there have been times when being able to call a tow-truck from AAA has been a lot more important than anything the NRA has ever done to secure my 2nd Amendment rights.

But the fact that I own a car doesn't make me any different from anyone else. And the fact that I am retired and drawing social security doesn't make me different from anyone else who was born before 1948. And despite the occasional "doom and gloom" that emanates from DC over the burden of entitlements, if you think the right to bear arms is sacred, try messing with that government check that I receive every month. So organizations like AAA and AARP do an effective job in reaching out to me and offering services that sometimes I really need. But neither of them make me feel special, or different because of who I am. That's where the NRA is way out in front.

But I'm getting ahead of myself here so let's go back fifty years to 1963, because this was the year that guns became, for the first time, an issue of public debate which would eventually transform itself into the current issue i.e., personal safety and security, which is what this book is all about. What happened in 1963 was that a Senator from Connecticut named Thomas Dodd introduced a gun bill in the wake of the assassination of JFK which was the first time that the government attempted to regulate gun ownership in a big way. The previous two national laws, passed in 1934 and 1938, regulated the ownership of automatic weapons, which nobody except Al Capone used anyway, and also imposed a few regulations on the conduct of gun dealers by defining to whom they could sell guns.

The bill that Dodd introduced in 1963 for the first time imposed restrictions on gun ownership for certain groups of individuals (felons, fugitives, etc.) and made it mandatory for the purchaser of a firearm from a licensed dealer to affirm that he or she was a resident in the state where the gun dealer was located, and that he/she was not prohibited under this law from owning a gun. But the law went beyond ownership based on legal qualifications because it also set standards for the manufacture and import of guns based on the government's belief that small, cheaply-made weapons were too often used in the commission of crimes. Such guns, known as "Saturday Night Specials," proliferated in poor neighborhoods, many of which were ghetto neighborhoods, and the phrase took on racist overtones in some of the public commentary surrounding the Dodd gun bill.

Actually, Dodd's motive for including prohibitions against the manufacture of these guns was probably more a function of concerns about the financial well-being of Connecticut gun makers like Winchester and Colt, but the net effect of this bill when it finally became law in 1968 was to put some gun manufacturers of the real cheapies out of business, one of whom was my Uncle Ben. He was actually my personal entrée into the gun business, but I'm getting a little ahead of myself.

My mother's family came to America from a *shtetl* in Eastern Europe between 1919 and 1921, and the original immigrant generation lived out their lives in and nearby their port of entry which happened to be

New York. The one outlier in the group was Uncle Ben, who ended up as a junk-metal purveyor in Rochester, NY and then before the War moved down South. He set up shop in Kinston, NC and went around salvaging metals under the name of the Imperial Metal Products Company, which was about as imperial or royal as my you-know-what. At some point he got into gun making and produced a small, cheaply-made 22-caliber revolver called the *IMP* (Imperial Metal Products, remember?) The gun sold retail in pawnshops and hardware stores for $29.95 but I think Ben turned them out for about 4 bucks apiece. Maybe the gun would fire one round before the cylinder broke in half or the barrel fell off, maybe not. But at a cost of four dollars, Ben could replace as many of them as he needed and still make a good profit from the little gun.

The GCA68 put Ben and lots of manufacturers like him smack out of business because the law required all guns to meet certain minimum manufacturing tolerances, including hardening of the steel, accuracy and so forth. You could still make a gun that was junky and cheap, but it couldn't be as cheap and junky as the *IMP*. So Ben stopped manufacturing guns and became the Smith & Wesson law enforcement distributor for North and South Carolina, a business I helped him run until he sold the whole thing to Sig Davidson in 1980 or 1981. Which is how and when I first got into the gun business, but I'm still getting ahead of myself.

The whole point about Saturday Night Specials was that this was the first time there was a debate about guns that connected them to crime and to race. There had been comments about guns and crime leading up to the laws passed by Roosevelt in 1934 and 1938, and these comments occasionally took on not so much racial, but ethnic overtones when Roosevelt's Attorney General Homer Cummings talked about taking guns away from "organized crime," which was a metaphor then and now for Americans of Italian descent. For that matter, the strict gun law known as the Sullivan Act, that was passed in New York City in 1911 and copied in other municipalities, was also aimed at keeping guns out of the hands of recent, less-civilized immigrants and other urban undesirables who were more or less likely to be from Italy's southern zones.

But when we drop the word "ethnic" and insert the word "race" we are talking about white versus black, and connecting guns to crimes committed by blacks was an argument that came out of the debates over GCA68 and remains with us to this day. There were two reasons that gave currency to the idea that too many black Americans were walking around with these little, cheap guns. First was the fact that anything that could be used to burnish the image of blacks as representing criminal threats to whites played well in many white areas, particularly in the South following the post-MLK assassination riots in 1968 and the white reaction to the steady expansion of civil rights. But the other reason had to do with the types of guns that most whites bought, owned and used, particularly whites with an interest in hunting or shooting sports,

As late as the 1960s, in fact into the 1970s, a majority of American gun owners had rifles, shotguns or both; at best one out of four privately-owned guns in America was a handgun, and the latter weapons were kept at home, worn outside only for reasons of work and almost never carried concealed for self-defense.[3] In fact, as late as the mid-1980s, 40 out of the 50 states either issued CCW (concealed-carry) on an extremely restricted basis or didn't issue CCW licenses at all. And while in some Southern states the bans on CCW were a legacy of Jim Crow laws, most of the non-issue states were in the West and the Midwest, a legacy of the old saloon dictum of "check 'em at the door."

Even if states had been more liberal in granting CCW, most gun owners would have been reluctant to walk around with a handgun because the size and weight of handguns being manufactured in the 1960s and 1970s made concealing such weapons uncomfortable or untenable at best. Handguns were manufactured out of steel, loaded with ammunition they weighed four pounds or more, and with the standard, four-inch or six-inch barrel they measured at least a foot in overall length. The American handgun was a legacy of the cowboy era, it then became standard equipment for the cops, but it wasn't something that could easily be carried around concealed, unless it was something cheap and small made by my Uncle Ben.

And if you think that the handguns were clunkers in the olden days, you should have seen the rifles. The rifle that could be found in just about every American farm home was either a lever-action Winchester, a bolt-action Remington or a cheap knock-off of one or the other from Sears. The guns were heavy, with wood stocks and metal receivers, and while auto-loading rifles with 5-shot magazines began sneaking into the civilian gun inventory in the '50s and '60s, they were never as popular (or as cheap) as their bolt-action counterparts. There were also military rifles floating around, in particular bolt-action Springfields that had seen service in both world wars and usually looked pretty beaten up, along with surplus Garands that came back from European arsenals in large numbers, many of which still had the original wooden stocks although most had been re-barreled because they were going to be used by European NATO forces who, by and large, refused to accept or use this old junk.

Along with the U.S.-made military guns, the civilian market also attracted increasing numbers of surplus rifles manufactured in European armories before World War I. Many of them came out of Turkey, there were also generous numbers of British Enfields with the "famed" .303 round. And after Japan surrendered and demobilized, there were gobs of Japanese Mauser-style rifles that also hit American shores. These guns were cheap, serviceable and often quite accurate; recall that Lee Harvey Oswald allegedly shot JFK with a surplus Mannlicher-Carcano of Italian origin that he bought from a Chicago import house for ten bucks. The import of the surplus military rifles spawned a whole cottage industry known as "sporterizing" guns, in which the original military stock would be replaced with a stock that made the gun look more like a hunting rifles, the iron sights would be replaced with a metal rail that could hold a scope, and the barrel would be polished inside and out to effect, so it was claimed, better shooting performance from the gun.

The 1968 GCA gave the ATF authority to determine whether an imported weapon was destined for "military" or "sporting" use, with the latter legally importable whereas the former had to stay off-shore. But this part of the law quickly became a dead letter by dint of simply importing the individual parts of the gun and assembling it over here. Gun entrepreneurs used the same flimflamming of the law to continue bringing in cheap, concealable handguns, a.k.a. the Saturday Night Specials, and it was one of these handguns, made in Germany by a company called RG but finished over here, that David Hinckley used when he tried to kill President ("Honey, I forgot to duck") Reagan in 1981.

With all due respect to George Patton's dictum that the M-1 Garand was the greatest battle implement ever devised, the truth is that, sporterized or not, military rifles were not really suited for sporting or hunting use. They tended to be heavy, had long barrels so as to create maximum energy when the bullet was released from the shell, and while young soldiers could carry them easily, once a hunter got to middle age, having to lug a heavy gun into the brush or up a tree just wasn't fun. The good news about the military guns is that for each caliber there tended to be a lot of cheap, foreign-made surplus ammo hanging around, so the cost of shooting those guns was considerably less than what someone would rack up bringing a box of new Remington, Winchester or Federal hunting ammunition out to the range.

Much of the ownership growth in surplus military guns after World War II was reflected in the development of another aspect of the gun industry known as handloading, or the assembly and use of self-made ammunition. Shotgunners frequently loaded their own ammunition because the ammo was nothing more than little, round lead balls which were simply stuffed into paper or brass (later plastic) cases, known as hulls; the brass or plastic cases able to be used multiple times. And since neither accuracy nor consistent performance were necessary in a smooth-bore barreled gun, shotgunners who were hunting or going to the trap/skeet range were frequently handloading ammunition in the decades prior to World War I.

Handloading centerfire ammunition however, particularly for high-powered rifles, didn't really get started until after World War II, and was first popularized by the Lyman Company, which started out making gunsights in the 1870s but then switched to reloading components in the 1920s and developed a full line of self-made ammunition tools sometime shortly after 1945. Centerfire reloading required more skill and expertise than shotshells because the bullet had to be seated properly in the shell for the ammo to work at all, plus the size of the powder charge had to be measured quite accurately so as to make sure that the pressures created by igniting the powder wouldn't be too small or too great for a particular caliber and gun.

I bought my first Lyman press, the tool that handloaders use to load and seal each round, in 1976 and I used it to load gobs of 45-caliber handgun ammo which I shot out of my 1911 Colt. I had picked up about five hundred rounds of brass from some shooting range that had gone out of business, the shells could be used again and again, and the good news about John Browning's masterpiece is that you didn't even have to measure the size of the powder charge as long as you could seat the bullet, tighten ("crimp") the shell and produce a round that would fit snugly into the magazine that was then inserted into the butt of the gun. It took me about 10 minutes to load 50 rounds, the only cost being the powder and the primer because I made the bullets by melting down lead wheel weights that I picked up off the floor of the local car garage.

When I really got into handloading, however, is when I happened to go out to sand pit where we used to go to shoot and bumped into something of a South

Carolina legend named Sherrill "SC" Smith. He was not only one of the most accomplished deer-hunters in the state, but was also acknowledged to load the best-performing handgun and rifle ammunition which, if he took a liking to you, he would sell you at a price far below what the stuff he made was really worth. I have to digress here for a second and mention the fact that while the gun industry is regulated more than any other consumer-product industry from end to end, the regulating kind of stops at your door front, particularly if you live in a Southern state where government regulations in general aren't greeted with hosannas in the first place.

If you want to manufacture guns, for example, you have to first acquire a Federal Firearms Manufacturers License, then you have to fill out and maintain all kinds of tax and inventory forms, then you have to let the ATF come nosing around when they have nothing better to do. Actually, you have to jump through all those hoops not to manufacture a gun, but to make it and then sell it to someone else. Because in order for any gun to move lawfully from a manufacturer to a wholesaler, a retailer or to another individual there has to be a record of the transaction along with a record of the serial number of the gun. But if you want to build a gun for yourself, you don't have to obey any kind of regulations at all. And this is true for ammunition which also requires a federal license and excise tax account in order to lawfully move the ammo from manufacturer to anyone else. But ammunition doesn't have serial numbers on the individual case, so if you want to scoop up some brass off the floor of the range, go home and reload it for another day, who's to tell whether or not you made it yourself or bought it from an ammunition maestro like Sherrill Smith?

Some of the ammunition loads that Sherrill made for me were astonishing in their accuracy and design. For example, he figured out that if you took a .357 magnum shell, loaded it to the crimp line with Hercules 2400 powder, which was used primarily for 30-06 rounds, then shot the load out of a 6-inch barreled revolver, you could line up a target 200 yards downrange and not have to worry about how much the bullet would drop. Because it wouldn't drop. We didn't have a chronograph so I couldn't really figure out the speed of that load, but there aren't many loads out there for any kind of hand gun that will shoot flat-on straight for anything over 100 yards. Oh yea, for all you trigger-heads reading this book I forgot to mention that the projectile was a 158-grain semi-wadcutter round which Sherrill molded himself. We would take some of this ammo, load it into a 6-inch nickel Colt Python that I owned, stick a hubcap up against a sandy hill, walk 200 yards away and see who could hit it 5 out of 6 shots. We knew we were on target when right after the gun went off we would hear a little "thunk." Couldn't see the round going through the hubcap, but we could hear whether our aim was right on or not.

The reason I'm going into this handloading business in such detail is because those of you who are gunnies like me will recognize what I'm talking about because you no doubt have had similar experiences with your own set of shooting friends. Those of you who aren't shooters will think I'm talking about the other side of the moon. And this is one of the issues, perhaps the most telling issue, which, when we think about guns, separates the two sides. Because if you like shooting, if you *really* like shooting and *really* like guns, you're not going to give it all up just because some nut walked into a schoolhouse with his AR-15 and blew the place apart. And the last thing you're going to do is let someone who *doesn't* know or like guns tell you what you can do with yours. That's not in the realm of possibility; it isn't even in the realm of impossibility.

But to get back to the narrative of this chapter, the point about handloading and guns in general is that shooting really was a hobby in the good old days, and nobody took seriously the idea that outside of bagging a deer with a rifle or going into the old sandpit with a revolver, that guns were meant for anything else. And don't fool yourself into believing that unless you lived in the South or on a farm or were in some way connected to America's rural past that shooting didn't have its pull. One of the most popular rifles ever produced was the Winchester 1890 slide-action rifle chambered for 22-caliber that was designed by none other than John Browning and patented in 1888. Known as a "gallery gun," because it could be found in every amusement park throughout the United States, I remember shooting one of them in Brooklyn's Coney Island probably in 1957 or 1958. So it didn't really matter whether you lived in the city or the country or somewhere in between, if you wanted to shoot a gun it wasn't difficult to find a venue where shooting, hunting or just old plain fooling around with a gun could take place.

The watershed moment in all of this benign gun stuff is usually thought to have occurred in 1977 when a former Immigration Service official from Texas named Harlon Carter started to run the NRA. The story has been told countless times about how Carter and some other Board members staged a coup at the annual meeting, booted out the old leadership and began spoiling for a fight with the government and anyone else who might oppose their *laissez-faire* attitude towards the regulation of guns. Some of the attitude of Carter and his supporters sprang from the degree to which the old leadership accommodated itself with many of the provisions of GCA68. But the real impetus behind the shift to a more aggressive posture reflected the growing strength of conservative political ideology and the extent to which that ideology was rooted in questions of crime and race.

For those who moved into adulthood over the last ten or twenty years, it might be difficult to imagine a time when the country defined so much of its politics and everyday culture in terms of race. But let's not forget that Ronald Reagan held his first, public campaign event in Philadelphia, MS, the town where sixteen years earlier Goodman, Cheney and Schwerner were executed, and his almost-nomination in 1976 symbolized a conservative resurgence that had been gradually building since the Goldwater debacle in 1964. And in the case of guns and gun laws, the anti-government mood in the South was readily apparent by 1968.

If we examine the voting on GCA68, a rather interesting picture emerges. In the House, of the 119 votes against the bill (306 voted in favor and a few didn't vote), the 13 Confederate states counted for 82, or more than two thirds of the opposition to the bill.

Most of the remaining negative votes came from the under-populated but traditionally pro-gun mountain states like Utah, Wyoming and Montana. The Senate, always more liberal than the House, only had 40% of the "nay" votes coming from the Confederacy, no doubt a reflection of the special arm-twisting talents of the former Senate leader who now occupied the White House.

Legislatively, the 1960's saw the imposition of federal laws on the South covering public access, voting rights and guns. In none of those instances did the South present a unified front against these laws because there were always some Southern liberals like Herman Talmadge, Thruston Morton and Albert Gore to counterbalance the likes of Stennis and Long. Guess where most of the negative votes came from when the House voted 292-132 to pass the civil rights bill in 1964? The same states where, four years later, you now had to fill out a federal form when you walked into a gun shop and bought a gun.

It wasn't difficult for Harlon Carter and his leadership group to begin selling the idea that the NRA had to start defending gun rights given the fact that two-thirds of the NRA membership, then and now, came from the same states whose elected officials lined up to vote against GCA68. The good news for the South in the 1970s is that if you switched party allegiances and voted Republican for the first time since before the Civil War, the occupant of the White House promised that he would "go slow" on civil rights. On the other hand, Nixon couldn't care less about guns or the people who liked having guns around. In fact, when Elvis met Nixon in the Oval Office because "The Pelvis" wanted a federal narcotics agent badge so that he could travel with his guns no matter where he went, Nixon agreed to a brief meeting even though he had no idea who Elvis was or why he would want to carry a gun.

It was the alignment of the NRA with the emerging "states' rights" strategy of national Republicanism that gave rise to the modern myth of guns being used for self-defense. But before I move forward with this narrative, let's briefly pause and consider the how and why of myths themselves. It is usually assumed that myths are based on traditions that go back in time to pre-modern days. But sometimes they are based simply on what we believe to be "universal" truths that are as important in contemporary culture as they were in times past. Myths are often sacred tales because in the Divine there is always a sense of justice and correctness. Myths are also ways of justifying the present by reference to an ancient and storied past. They can also be used as a contemporary frame of reference to explain changes perceived to be threatening if not exactly understood.

The myth of self-defense that grew up and was promoted about guns embodies all these ideas. First and foremost it is rooted in the so-called "Biblical" injunction of "an eye for an eye," and remember that most of the gun-rich regions also fall within the Bible belt. Second, it is above being questioned because even though Jesus spoke of turning the other cheek, the idea of protecting hearth and home embodies the basic importance of family and friends. And finally, self-defense became a response to the fears and insecurities engendered by the racial turbulence of the 1960s and 1970s which, particularly in the South, fused fears about civil rights with fears about crime.

Under the leadership of Harlon Carter, the NRA began to promote the idea that gun control, particularly as it was practiced at the federal level, was not only another example of federal usurpation of local and states' rights, but would also result in the disarming of Americans who needed guns to protect themselves from crime (read: Blacks.) And if anyone for one minute doubted the degree to which the NRA and lots of other Americans began to equate crime with race, NRA television ads featuring Charlton Heston made this point about as explicitly as it could be made. The spots showed a dark and gritty street in DC, obviously somewhere in the ghetto with the dome of the Capitol far off in the distance and Heston saying something about how politicians could sleep comfortably in their beds but the "average" resident feared for his life. Get it?

But while the NRA was slowly expanding and mobilizing its base to support a much more politicized agenda, in practical terms the organization really didn't push its pro-2nd Amendment message with any degree of strength or certainty throughout the Reagan years. This was largely due to the fact that Reagan may have not let a day go by without reminding everyone that he was the leader of the conservative movement, even though his leadership rarely was on display for the niche social issues like abortion and guns that his conservative followers, particularly in the evangelical movement, wanted to call their own.

In the case of guns, for example, Reagan signed the 1986 *Firearm Owners Protection Act*, loudly supported by the NRA, which reigned in some of the abuses of GCA68 and also liberalized the movement of long guns across state lines. That same year he also signed the *Law Enforcement Officers Protection Act* which banned certain kinds of surplus military ammunition, a law that the NRA quietly opposed. The NRA opposed LEOPA because it restricted .223 ammunition that could be used for target practice and hunting small game, but the opposition was muted by the fact that LEOPA was supported by the cops who believed that certain types of surplus .223 ammunition could slice through protective vests. Ultimately, LEOPA passed both the House and the Senate on a rarely-used, non-recorded voice vote, a shrewd parliamentary maneuver that allowed many pro-NRA House and Senate members to claim to be pro-gun while being pro-cop as well.

One might compare what happened with LEOPA when the ATF attempted to ban another type of surplus 223 ammo in 2015. This time around the new regulations again received the support of official police groups, but there was an avowedly progressive anti-gun guy in the White House with whom the NRA was always spoiling for a fight, and the efforts by the ATF to get rid of another type of "cop-killing" ammo (i.e., allegedly it could pierce an armor vest) went right down the drain, along with the tenure of the ATF Director, who had been on the job for less than two years.

The world of gun advocacy changed dramatically when Bill Clinton took office in 1992. In fact, it can be said that gun advocacy in its current iteration first emerged in the years 1993-94, when the Administration pushed two gun bills through Congress, the first known as the Brady Bill, and the second known as the Assault Weapons Ban which was part of the crime bill that went through just before Clinton lost his Democratic House and Senate majorities at the end of 1994. Both of these bills represented statutory initiatives that had been introduced years earlier but remained dead letters while the White House was occupied first by Reagan and then Bush. But the appearance of a Southern, activist liberal at 1600 Pennsylvania Avenue with Democratic majorities in both legislative chambers had not been seen since Lyndon Johnson left office shortly after affixing his signature to GCA68.

The gun laws signed by Clinton in 1994 went far beyond anything that was different between the gun bill passed under Roosevelt in 1938 and the bill passed under Johnson in 1968. The one major difference between 1938 and 1968 was that the latter statute created a regulatory framework for all federal gun matters and a regulatory agency, a.k.a. the ATF. But the 1968 law did not regulate end-user purchases to any great degree because even though an over-the-counter customer had to affirm that he did not fall into any of the "prohibited" gun-owning categories, his statement at the time of purchase was usually accepted by the dealer as fact. And while the dealer had to substantiate that he and the purchaser were located in the same state, in fact this had also been required by the law passed in 1938.

GCA68 also did not change in any ways the types of guns that non-prohibited persons could buy or own. It did set a new requirement for the types of materials that had to be used in the manufacture of guns, but this was an attempt to drive the cheaply-made, Saturday Night Specials out of the market, most of which were imported from overseas. The NRA didn't find these new manufacturing regulations to be particularly onerous and, with the exception of my Uncle Ben, neither did anyone else. In sum, the gun-owning environment that emerged after GCA68 did not change much at all.

The 1994 Clinton bills, on the other hand, substantially altered the regulatory landscape to the degree that they were bound to provoke loud and angry opposition from the NRA. The Brady bill, passed early in the year, took responsibility for attesting to legal status out of the hands of the purchaser or the dealer and vested it with the ATF and FBI. The bill required that no gun could be transferred by a dealer to a customer unless the individual to whom the gun was being transferred was first approved by the FBI. This meant a telephone call to a call center in West Virginia where the staff had access to a national database which could be checked against the personal identifiers of the individual receiving the gun. If the individual in question appeared on any list of the various prohibited categories, the gun could not be put in his hands.

The Assault Weapons Ban, which was tacked onto the crime bill and passed just before the Democrats lost their majorities in both the Senate and the House, was also a major change in the regulatory environment because, for the first time, the government was stepping in to tell Americans what kinds of guns they could actually own. Ironically, the ban didn't really cover the sale or ownership of what we refer to as "assault weapons" today, namely, AR-15 rifles manufactured by the likes of Bushmaster,

Panther Arms, Colt and Stag. It did, however, ban a number of products if the gun in question was a semi-automatic weapon and was built or could accept two or more of the five following accessories: folding stock, bayonet lug, flash suppressor, grenade launcher or pistol grip.

Along with these design limitations, which applied both to long guns and hand guns, no type of weapon, no matter how designed, could be sold as a new gun if it came with a magazine holding more than ten rounds. How anyone could ever imagine that a rifle with a screw on the side of the barrel which allowed someone to attach a bayonet was *ipso facto* more lethal with or without a hi-capacity magazine simply boggles my mind. For that matter, if I had been a stand-up comic back in those days, I can guarantee you I would have figured out a monologue in which I would explain to my audience in the most mock seriousness why banning grenade launchers made such perfect sense.

The one provision of the bill which did make sense in terms of limiting the lethality of these guns was the ban on hi-capacity magazines which covered civilian but exempted law enforcement sales. You would think that in the aftermath of this legislation the government would have created some kind of research activity to determine whether any of these changes in gun design had any effect on what the law was designed to do; namely, cut down on gun violence and, in particular, gun violence caused by these types of guns. But what the government then did, two years after the ban went into effect, was to drop all funding on gun research, leading the Department of Justice in 2004 to conclude that there hadn't been enough research conducted on the results of the assault weapons ban to see whether it had worked or not.

I want to pause the narrative again at this point and make a comment about the NICS. There has been a lot of back and forth about the value of NICS in terms of to what degree the background check, admittedly only covering over-the-counter sales, makes much of a difference in terms of keeping guns out of the wrong hands. The pro-gun community looks at the paltry number of indictments that grow out of falsifying NICS information and claims that the system really doesn't change anything at all. The gun-control community notes that every year the number of denials goes down, indicating that the system increasingly prevents the bad guys from even thinking about going into a gun shop and purchasing a gun.

I happen to think that both arguments say nothing really important about the degree to which

NICS has altered the regulatory landscape for guns within the United States. To me, the value of the NICS system was that it forced many states which previously had underdeveloped and chaotic licensing systems to bring their efforts at regulating guns up to speed. For example, in my state, Massachusetts, the appearance of NICS forced the state to overhaul its own licensing process which, despite a required permit that had to be issued before someone bought a gun, in many towns and localities didn't exist at all.

In Massachusetts the issuing authority, a.k.a. the local chief, had to send the paperwork plus fingerprints and photos to an office in Boston which then allegedly checked court records, sent the results of that check to the State Police who then sent an "approve" or "deny" order back to the local chief. If the local chief received an "approve" for a particular application, he or someone else sat down and manually typed out the license on a piece of heavy paper which, after being carried around in a wallet, usually turned into shreds. But in many towns, particularly smaller localities, the chief personally knew just about everyone who wanted to own or buy a gun. So why bother to even send in the application to Boston when you know the applicant has never done anything wrong? You think I'm kidding but I'm not when I say that hundreds if not thousands of gun licenses were handled this way not just in Massachusetts but other states as well. I knew a county sheriff in South Carolina who not only gave out gun licenses without any kind of paperwork, but would also sell the new license-holder a gun out of the collection of confiscated weapons that he had accumulated over the years.

By standardizing databases and application procedures all over the country, the NICS represented another example of federal intrusion into local affairs. Which was exactly what residents in gun-rich states, particularly below the Mason-Dixon line, resented most of all. And with all due respect to the gun-control community and their concerns for guns getting into the wrong hands, the fact is that no law-abiding person who ever bought or owned a gun imagined that it would be one of *his* guns that ended up being used in a violent crime. So to the extent that social niche issues continued to play a prominent role in defining the contours of the red versus blue political landscape from the passage of Brady and the Assault Weapons Ban and beyond, the NRA quickly moved to consolidate its ownership of one of those issues, the gun issue, for which, ironically, it was a gun company combined with the Clinton Administration that gave the NRA a powerful helping hand.

The same year that GCA68 was passed, the last surviving relative of D. B. Wesson died and the ownership and management of the storied gun company moved into non-family hands. The company was purchased by a conglomerate called *Bangor Punta,* whose main holding was *Piper Aircraft* which certainly had nothing to do with guns. Things then stumbled along until 1987 when *Bangor Punta,* now owned by *Lear Siegler,* sold *Smith & Wesson* to a British holding company, *Tompkins, PLC.* S&W was now owned by a British conglomerate which attempted to build a collection of companies specializing in mechanical consumer goods, their other major acquisition being a company that made cheap bicycles for Sears.

A few years after *Bangor Punta* purchased *Smith & Wesson,* the near-virtual monopoly that S&W enjoyed over the commercial handgun market began to wither away and die. This was because the U.S. Army decided in 1977 to shelve the venerable Colt 1911 pistol and replace it with a high-capacity, double-action pistol and, after several years of field tests, ultimately selected the Beretta 92. The moment that the military gave its blessing to a 9mm pistol as its official sidearm, police departments around the country began shifting to European, hi-cap pistols from *Beretta, Glock* and *Sig,* and the American cop market which Smith had wrested away from Colt after World War II was now in foreign hands.

Law enforcement and tax-exempt sales in general had never accounted for more than 20% of *Smith & Wesson* revenues, the company then and now was dependent on commercial or what was known as sporting-goods sales. But what the cops carried was a major factor in determining civilian preferences in handguns, so as Beretta, Sig and Glock began to take over the police market, their share of the sporting goods market climbed as well.

Believe it or not, *Smith & Wesson's* catalog actually contained a hi-cap, polymer frame, double-action 9mm pistol known as the Model 59. The gun had gone into production in the 1960s when the S&W engineering department very innovatively began to think about competing with the European pistol makers for military and law enforcement contracts outside the U.S. There was only one little problem with the Model 59, which is why it failed not one but two Army field tests that were conducted to find a replacement for John Browning's Colt. The little problem was that the gun didn't work.

Well, it kind of worked except that when the slide locked back after firing the last shot, and a new, loaded magazine was then slapped into the grip and the slide release lever was lowered so that the slide would move forward and push the first round into the breech, the hammer had a funny habit of dropping down on the firing pin as the slide moved forward and – *boom!* – the gun would go off. The other problem with the gun was that if you removed the slide from the frame in order to clean the inside of the gun, you really had to be a rocket scientist to figure out how to reassemble the gun so that it would shoot. Reassembling it so that it wouldn't work wasn't very difficult; the trick was to put it back together and be able to load, aim and fire again.

What kept Smith in the game in the 70s and 80s were innovations in the design and manufacture of revolvers, including stainless-steel construction, concealable, lightweight back-up guns and the N-frame big magnums, in particular the Model 29, a.k.a. the Dirty Harry 44-magnum, which remained on back-order for years after Clint Eastwood first said, "make my day," even though he actually didn't say it until the movie *Sudden Impact* that was released in 1983. These revolver models were distinctly *Smith & Wesson* and kept the company name in the forefront of the industry even though each year the hi-cap pistols coming in from Europe were gaining an increasing amount of market share. Perhaps it was the increasing competition from pistol makers, no matter how many new revolver products the company rolled out; perhaps it was the foreign ownership which, by definition, didn't really understand very much about guns; perhaps it was just a stupid mistake. Whatever it was, the decision by *Smith & Wesson* to break ranks with the rest of the gun industry and make a deal with the government in terms of how it sold and distributed its guns gave the NRA a stature within and without the gun world that it never lost.

What happened was that, as an outgrowth of a series of class-action litigation against gun makers, the Clinton Administration began to negotiate the development of a series of self-regulating safety and sales procedures for the gun industry to follow which would then exempt the industry from the threat of federal suits. The talks, which went on sporadically throughout 1998-99, ended abruptly on March 1, 2000 when *Smith & Wesson* broke ranks with the industry and announced that it had voluntarily agreed to make a deal with the White House and adopt a new set of policies for distributing and selling its guns.

The new policies were a wish-list of just about everything that a gun-control advocate could desire, including mandatory waiting periods on purchases, safety training for consumers and dealers, setting aside revenue for smart-gun technologies and safe-gun marketing campaigns, creating a "watchdog" committee to insure compliance with the new rules, and keeping minors out of any gun shop sales area unless accompanied by an adult. The agreement also covered physical security at gun shops (guns had to be locked away) and in gun factories, including installation of anti-theft devices and background checks on drivers whose trucks delivered guns from factories to wholesale houses and dealer locations. In other words, it was crazy and, for the most part unenforceable.

Within a few days after the deal was announced, gun dealers and even some wholesalers began shipping guns back to Springfield and the internet was peppered with anti-S&W comments coming from all sides. Three weeks after the deal was announced, when it was clear that gun-owning opinion was running strongly against the agreement, the NRA began to make angry, public statements about the Smith & Wesson "sellout" and joined with the NSSF to keep other gun makers from following Smith's lead. What turned the tide in the gun industry's favor was the announcement by *RSR*, a national wholesaler which probably sold one out of every five S&W guns, that they would stop doing business with the Springfield factory because the terms of the agreement aimed at distributors were too "onerous" for *RSR* to meet and comply.

Had the deal between the government and S & W actually gone through, and had the government tried to enforce it, and had the agreement then spread to other gun companies, all of whom would have been sitting ducks for class-action torts if they didn't get in line, there is no question in my mind that the commercial manufacture and sale of guns in the United States might have been dealt a serious, if not game-ending blow. Because what the agreement called for was to force *Smith & Wesson* to be responsible for the behavior and business practices of thousands of retail resellers, none of whom had any direct relationship to the manufacturer at all, but all of whom ultimately were responsible for getting more than ninety percent of the company's products into the civilian market, thus controlling the gun company's financial destiny from afar.

Traditionally, guns have always been sold to the consumer through a two-tier distribution system; the manufacturer sells to a wholesaler, the wholesaler sells to the retailer and the retailer then makes over-the-counter sales. Back in the 1980s, when S & W began to feel competitive pressure from pistol manufacturers like *Beretta, Sig* and *Glock,* for the first time ever the company decided to go out and set up a dealer program to encourage retailers to stock and sell more of their guns. Smith had been the dominant player in the commercial, or as it was called the "sporting goods" market after World War II because just about every cop in America carried a K-frame, *Smith & Wesson* gun. And to the degree that the civilian taste in handguns basically followed whatever the cops tended to carry, owning virtually the entire law enforcement market meant that Smith controlled the sporting goods market as well.

On the sporting goods side of the factory in Springfield, S & W pumped out 200,000 guns each year, but virtually all of them were sold to 30-32 national wholesalers who then resold them to retailers in whatever regional market the particular wholesaler tended to operate here and there. All of a sudden, after the Army picked the *Beretta* and *Glock* started giving its guns away to the cops, Smith found itself in the unenviable position of not only losing the law enforcement market, which had never accounted for more than a quarter of sales, but facing a diminishing sporting goods presence as well. So they hired a marketing firm which went out and did a very detailed survey of the type of dealer who sold S & W guns, and then decided that if a retailer stocked their products and sold at least one gun a week (i.e., 50 a year), they would consider this store to be a "key" dealer, festoon the place with posters and various countertop doodads, rebate a percentage of the dealer's advertising when *Smith & Wesson* was mentioned in the ads, and basically build a loyal network of retailers to whom the wholesalers, over time, would ship more guns.

There was only one little problem with this program. When all was said and done, the company discovered that its point of sale network was exceedingly wide but very thin. There were gun dealers all over the place, many of whom, particularly in the South, tended to be pawn shops, and only a small percentage could be considered as stocking enough guns of any manufacturer to be called retailers in the usual way that we use that word. Many of the dealers worked out of their homes or their garages, others had s small gun case in the back of the hardware or dry goods store; guns tended to be expensive items so the retailer was often happy to forego the extra profit in return for letting the wholesalers hold and pay for the inventory until they ordered up a specific gun. And since guns were always shipped overnight delivery for security and safety reasons, and since wholesalers would normally ship to anyone who held a valid FFL, most gun dealers avoided holding onto inventory like the plague, knowing that they could fill a customer order within a couple of days.

Given this hodge-podge situation at the retail level, it is inconceivable to me that a company like *Smith & Wesson,* which operated at best on a gross margin of under 30%, could have ever absorbed the costs of regulating and supervising the behavior of its retail dealer base. Particularly because, the way the agreement was worded, any retailer who actually received and resold a new *Smith & Wesson* product fell under the regulatory infrastructure that the company was promising to develop and maintain.

Looking back at the agreement that *Smith & Wesson* signed, which then became a dead letter when the company was sold and, more to the point, when some Gore-Lieberman votes in Palm Beach County never saw the light of day, was the degree to which many of the safety requirements contained in the agreement are now followed by the gun industry without the slightest degree of inconvenience or protest. For example, the agreement requires that all handguns be shipped with an external locking device, which the Bush Administration mandated in 1995. Handguns also must have two serial numbers, one of them in an internal location that cannot be seen unless the gun is disassembled, which is a requirement in certain states and is followed by all manufacturers as well as importers of handguns. Many pistols are also sold now with magazine disconnectors (which means the gun will not fire unless the magazine is in place) and a loaded chamber indicator, also stipulated in the agreement, is standard on many pistols manufactured today.

But the difference between the industry's adoption of those safety devices and the Clinton-S&W agreement was that the gun maker was basically allowing the government to exercise a degree of regulation over sales, marketing and gun access that went far beyond anything in the Brady and assault weapons bills. And the fact that the pushback against this agreement was, if not led then at least heavily promoted by the NRA, made the organization the *de facto* torchbearer for both gun makers and gun owners; in other words, for the gun community as a whole. Legend and self-promotion to the contrary, the NRA never actually called for an official boycott of *Smith & Wesson*. But through their media and public relations reach they were able to appear to be leading both the charge against the gun maker as well as being the chief defender of the gun industry as a whole. When *Tompkins, PLC* divested itself of *Smith & Wesson* in 2001 for about 15% of what they paid to acquire the company fourteen years earlier, the idea that the NRA could determine the business fortunes of America's most famous gun maker became fixed in the public's mind. More important, the NRA could argue that it was truly the gun industry's best friend and protector, which meant that any argument it wanted to make about guns, such as the argument for armed self-defense, would become gospel in the consciousness of the pro-gun community and all gun fans.

The fact that within nine months after the boycott ended the gun industry found itself with a friend, rather than an enemy in the White House only helped the NRA to consolidate its leadership role. The Bush Administration, sensitive to the needs of its large coalition of niche voters, went out of its way to reward the NRA and its gun-owning followers by scrapping the entire federal litigation effort involving guns, eliminating CDC-sponsored gun-research funding, restricting access to ATF tracing data and FBI NICS checks, and cloaking the industry in a protective shield against class-action liability torts.

There was one gun-control initiative sponsored by Clinton, however, which the Bush Administration not only didn't reverse, but actually strengthened in 2003. And this had to do with the import of guns from China, which had been partially blocked by Clinton in 1993. The issue involved a Chinese company known as *Norinco*, which manufactured a wide array of defense-related products, including small arms that were of surprisingly high quality and, like many imported Chinese products, came into the U.S. at a favorable consumer price. In particular, *Norinco* made a copy of the Colt 1911 pistol known as the M1911-A1 and an AK-47 rifle, known as the Model 56. I owned a Model 56 a few years back, and it was superior in quality and performance to any of the Middle European AKs that came in from Rumania, Czechoslovakia, Serbia or points further East. The decision by the Bush Administration to stop all *Norinco* gun imports had nothing to do with protecting the American market; it was based on the fact that the parent company back in China may have sold nuclear technology to Iran.

When the import ban was announced there was a bit of grumbling from the usual gaggle of 2nd-Amendment absolutists who were crawling all over the web, but there wasn't even a small stink coming from the NRA. And maybe they knew it and maybe they didn't, but this decision by the Bush Administration was the biggest gift given by Bush to the American gun manufacturers of all. Because the truth is that had China been allowed to continue bringing small arms into the U.S. market, and had those products, like most Chinese products now sold in America, been copies of what we were making over here, there is no way that American gun makers could have competed with the Chinese in terms of quality or price.

While the G.W. Bush administration did the gun industry a big favor by not reversing the *Norinco* decision, they did the industry a bigger favor by allowing the Clinton-S&W agreement to become a dead letter, thus consolidating the prestige of the NRA in the eyes of gun owners, as well as defining a basic political alliance between the pro-gun community and the GOP. The NRA became increasingly politically active both at the federal and state levels, the latter venues becoming the environments for the near-total expansion of concealed-carry laws and the former venue, in particular the Federal court system, for the growth and eventual triumph of the self-defense rationale for the 2nd Amendment as expressed in the Heller decision handed down in 2008.

The decision by the NRA and other pro-gun advocates to promote gun ownership for protection against crime pulled the industry away from its reliance on sport and hunting products and pushed it towards the development and marketing of defensive handgun and tactical long guns which now define the industry's product and advertising profile as a whole. Whether the gun industry promoted armed defense which was then picked up by the NRA, or whether it was the NRA which first pushed the issue and provided the gun industry a new rationale for the purchase of guns is probably a classic chicken-and-egg situation for which I suspect both explanations bear some degree of truth. The one thing that didn't happen as a result of this new definition of gun use was any real degree of increase in the number of Americans who owned guns. In absolute numbers there probably was a small growth in the size of the gun-owning population, but this was a reflection of the continued growth of the country's population as a whole. In fact, the proportion of people living in the United States who owned guns probably reached a high water-mark sometime before World War II, when a majority of Americans were still living in farm communities or smaller towns.

But the fact that a smaller and smaller percentage of Americans would own guns had nothing to do with the growth of the myth that Americans needed guns to protect themselves from crime. And this myth of the "armed citizen" would not only become the rationale for the spread of laws that now enable most adult Americans to walk around with guns, it was also the myth that became the ultimate rationale for the 2008 *Heller* decision which definitively extended a Constitutional protection over personal ownership and, more important, use of guns. This entire change in the culture of guns from how they were made to how and whom they would be sold came about because gun owners embraced the "armed citizen" myth. And what I will now explain is how the change came about.

CHAPTER 2

ORIGINS OF THE MYTH

It's usually assumed that guns were a staple of everyday life from the moment that white settlers first began to hack away at the forests and woodland that could be found just beyond the sandy beaches of the East Coast. But what really happened almost from the very first settlement s was an attempt by colonial governments to control the use and commerce of guns. The very first time that a group of colonists actually sat down to write a set of laws, the Virginia Assembly in 1619, one of the laws that was passed prohibited the sale or transfer of firearms to Indians for the simple reason that such weapons could then be turned against the settlers who, in many instances, weren't particularly welcome on these new shores.[1]

Notice that right from the git-go, gun control laws were basically designed to keep guns out of the "wrong hands," in this case, hands of Native Americans who presented, by definition, a threat to public order in the colonies. In the period between 1619 and 1790, a.k.a. the colonial era, laws that restricted who could own guns and how they could be used were passed by virtually every colonial administration in every colony, including laws that specifically prohibited gun ownership by felons and non-residents.

The largest number of gun control laws, of course, related to issues involving guns that residents had to furnish when they appeared for militia duty. I'll talk about this issue in depth in Chapter 4, when I discuss how the "sacred text" of the armed citizen came to be developed; in the meantime, it just needs to be noted that the legislative activity surrounding gun control was initiated almost from the beginning of the country itself, and was motivated primarily by a desire of colonial administrations to make sure that community, as opposed to personal defense could be met by using firearms.

But firearms during and after the colonial period were usually considered to be long guns, which of course were essential for arming the militia, as well as for protection and hunting in wilderness zones. Handguns, on the other hand, were, generally speaking, considered to be offensive and dangerous in normal everyday affairs, particularly after the 1804 duel between Alexander Hamilton and Aaron Burr which cost the first Secretary of the Treasury his life. In fact, at the same time that States were inserting guarantees for gun ownership into their own Constitutions, many were also outlawing concealed-carry of handguns, a legal restriction that could be found in virtually every state or territory before the nineteenth century came to an end.

As for the OK Corral and also those other legendary gun fights (and gun fighters) of the Old West, the historian Richard Shenkman sums it up best in his study of Western towns when he says that, "many more people have died in Hollywood westerns than ever died on the real frontier. In the most violent year in Deadwood, South Dakota, only four people were killed. In the worst year in Tombstone, home of the shoot-out at the OK Corral, only five people were killed. The only reason the OK Corral shoot-out even became famous was that town boosters deliberately overplayed the drama to attract new settlers."[2]

I find it ironic that in the present-day argument over guns, the pro-gun folks often portray the movie industry as being opposed to gun ownership, a function of the fact that the entertainment industry, with a few notable exceptions (read: Ronald Reagan among others) is decidedly liberal in its core political beliefs, which means that every four years the industry gives most of its financial support to the

Democratic presidential candidate who always turn out to be anti-gun. In his strident defense of gun ownership after the massacre at Sandy Hook, Wayne LaPierre energized his followers by reminding them that "a child growing up in America today witnesses 16,000 murders, and 200,000 acts of violence by the time he or she reaches the ripe old age of 18. And, throughout it all, too many in the national media, their corporate owners, and their stockholders act as silent enablers, if not complicit co-conspirators."[3]

Of course what Wayne forgot to mention was that these same corporate owners have been busily creating entertainment for more than a century which again and again shows "good guys" protecting us from "bad guys" by using a gun. In fact, what is often considered to be the first, modern movie with real action, *The Great Train Robbery*, was made in 1903, and in 1990 was declared by none other than the Library of Congress as "culturally, historically, and aesthetically significant." And what was the plot of this ten-minute film? A bunch of bad guys and a bunch of good guys blasting away at each other with guns.

The most famous, or infamous gun-control law depending on your point of view, was New York City's Sullivan Law that took effect in 1911, a law which with only minor changes remains in use to this day. The law was passed at the insistence of a local politician, Timothy Sullivan, and basically it gave the New York City Police Department wide discretion over who could own and carry a concealable gun. Not only did the law require that an applicant pass a background check in order to purchase and own a handgun, it also mandated that every handgun could only be purchased with the issuance of a purchase permit covering that particular weapon, and that following receipt of the gun from a dealer, the owner then had to allow the NYPD licensing division to inspect and approve the specific gun itself.

I owned a bunch of handguns when I lived in New York City during throughout the 1980s, and the purchase of every single gun required two separate trips downtown to the Licensing Division with waits that averaged between three and four hours each time, and rarely was I able to get down there in time to actually find an empty chair. The entire gun licensing area, which occupied half of the first floor of NYPD's headquarters building two blocks away from City Hall, was the province of a fearsome, little old lady named Mrs. Skiba, who as far as I knew didn't have a first name. She had an assistant, Jose, who had a first name but no last name, or at least no last name that was ever said out loud. And in those days there were no computers so all the data covering every legal gun in New York City was crammed into rows and rows of metallic-grey filing cabinets which took up most of the space on the floor.

So here's what would happen when you ventured into Mrs. Skiba's domain. First you had to get on line and wait until you got up to her desk. You didn't take a number, you didn't register with a receptionist, you stood there and waited until it was your turn. Then you told Mrs. Skiba who you were and why you had come down to the Licensing Division and Mrs. Skiba would then yell out your last name and a minute or so later Jose would come trundling up to her desk holding a manila folder that contained all of the documentation about you and all your guns. Incidentally, Mrs. Skiba rarely asked anyone standing in front of her desk for ID because legend had it that there wasn't a single license-holder in the city of New York who actually predated the time when Mrs. Skiba was put in charge of the giving out licenses for guns.

I once showed up on a day when, for some crazy reason, Mrs. Skiba chose not to appear. So everyone stood around for a couple of hours and then we all went home. I was lucky because on that occasion I happened to be running a gun wholesaling operation that was located just a few blocks away from where Mrs. Skiba held court. At least I didn't have to spend an hour or more on the subway coming in from The

Bronx or Queens in order to learn that I had wasted a day because Mrs. Skiba wasn't sitting behind her desk.

The good news about owning a handgun in New York City was that if you met the legal requirements and were willing to put up with Mrs. Skiba's nonsense, your license was issued without a hitch, most purchase orders for additional handguns were processed quickly and the license was renewed through the mail, thus avoiding a further trip down to "Number One" as it was called unless you wanted to purchase another gun. It should also be pointed out that the process of getting licensed to own and purchase shotguns and rifles was in those days a very simple and expedient affair. One filled out an application, enclosed a check and a set of prints and a month or so later you received a long gun license which allowed you to purchase and own as many rifles and shotguns as you could stuff into your apartment closets without ever having to go near the NYPD or Mrs. Skiba at all. In fact, the long gun license was issued by something known as the Firearms Control Board, which was located somewhere out in Queens next to the police garage where all the car radios were repaired. So owning a long gun in New York City was hardly different from a licensing perspective than owning a shot gun or rifle just about anywhere else. But when it was a question

of a handgun, particularly if you wanted to carry a
pistol or revolver on your person, the Sullivan Law
applied and this was an entirely different kettle of fish.

I was qualified to carry a concealed handgun
because for several years I managed a security
company that supplied unarmed and armed guards to
commercial enterprises as well as to VIPs. And since
on occasion I acted as the bodyguard to some big-
shot or another (once I was actually part of a trio that
shlepped around Manhattan with Donald Trump), the
NYPD authorized me to carry a gun. But I could only
carry the gun when I was doing something which
actually required having a gun on my person, and I
had to register that one gun only with Mrs. Skiba and
the NYPD. The good news for me was that somehow
Mrs. Skiba got it in her head that I was a personal
employee of Trump, so whenever I walked into her
domain at the Licensing Division I immediately was
told to come to the head of the line.

On the other hand, I had a friend who owned a
travel agency in midtown Manhattan, and for
whatever reason many of his customers paid him in
cash. So he actually carried large sums of money,
often tens of thousands of dollars, between his office
and the bank. He applied for, and eventually received
a concealed-carry handgun license based on business
"need," but it took him six months to accumulate

enough deposit slips showing continuous cash deposits before he was approved to carry a gun.

One day this friend of mine happened to leave his office at the end of a workday, got in his car and started to drive home to Long Island. On his way home he hit a traffic jam in Brooklyn on the Belt Parkway, pulled the car into a parking area and decided to wait out the jam by taking a brief walk. Maybe he was 100 yards from his car when all of a sudden a large and fierce dog ran up and began nipping at his heels and then tried to bite his leg. At which point David pulled out his gun and shot the dog dead. Thirty seconds later a cop car pulled up, then a second, then a third. Ultimately David was allowed to proceed on his way but he first had to surrender the gun (this is an absolutely true story) so that the NYPD forensics lab could test and make sure that the bullet recovered from the gun was the same gun that David was licensed to carry within the City of New York.

I am relating this story of David the dog-killer because it reflects the degree to which gun control, when taken to the extreme, can produce results that have nothing to do with why laws are passed to control guns. But suffice it to say that while the Sullivan Law may still make it virtually impossible for the average New York City resident to walk around with a legal gun, this was, to a greater or lesser extent, the situation regarding concealed-carry that existed in most states and localities from the founding of the country until 1987 when Florida changed its concealed-carry law from "may issue" to "shall issue" and, in the process, set in motion the modern wave of concealed-carry laws that now make the concept of the "armed citizen" a reality in just about every locality and state.

The concealed-carry law passed in Florida marked the first time the NRA began using its political and financial muscle to make changes in the legal environment surrounding guns at the state level. The gun organization actually only began a legal lobbying effort in 1975, when it created a new initiative known as the Institute for Legislative Action (ILA) whose efforts were initially aimed at Capitol Hill. But what the NRA quickly began to understand was that while the 2nd Amendment was something of an iconic representation of gun rights, the real battle for legal gun ownership would take place at the state level because it was state legislatures who possessed the authority to regulate consumer items of all kinds, not just guns. And when Florida became one of the early states to mandate seat belts on January 1, 1986, anyone who knew anything about gun control had to believe that state gun legislation might not be far behind.

Enter Marian Hammer, a Florida native who started running an NRA front organization known as *Unified Sportsmen of Florida* in 1976. Neither she nor this organization made any attempt to disguise the fact that they supported and were supported by the NRA. It really just had to do with the legalities of federal lobbying laws which required the NRA to create some distance between its federal lobbying effort and efforts to make changes in state laws. The one thing that Marian Hammer and other pro-gun folks had going for them at the state level was the fact that the gun-control community in those days had no effective local activity at all. Which meant that, if nothing else, state gun laws could be modified to more closely reflect the NRA agenda without facing much opposition from anti-gun activists who simply weren't there.

What really opened up the playing field for the NRA and other pro-gun activists to move forward on concealed-carry laws was the fact that the late 1980s coincided with a growth in public concern about crime. And it wasn't crime per se that created this concern, but crime as it appeared to be perpetrated by minority, inner-city youths, an attitude that spread through the middle class particularly after the "subway shooting" committed by Bernard Goetz in 1984 and the Los Angeles riots which followed the 1992 not-guilty verdict of the cops who beat up Rodney King.

Goetz was a computer engineer who lived in Manhattan and found himself being menaced one night on the subway by a group of young Black men. The group started taunting Goetz, he pulled out a gun, fired five times and wounded four, one of whom would be paralyzed for the remainder of his life. Goetz was found innocent of the assault charges and became something of a cult hero, particularly among gun advocates who were promoting concealed-carry in numerous states.

As for Los Angeles, what made the riot so remarkable in terms of how it galvanized feelings about the "threat" of crime was partially the fact that it took place at the end of a half-decade of unprecedented increase in violent crime during which the national crime rate soared by more than one-third in the period 1985-1992. I was living in New York City at the time, and I recall that people really believed that city streets were *verboten* for walking after 6 P.M., restaurants closed early so that the help didn't have to travel home on the subways late at night, and you couldn't stop for a traffic light anywhere in Manhattan without a gang of rough-looking characters coming up to the car and demanding money whether they washed your windshield or not. I once had my front windshield washed four times driving across 86th Street from Madison Avenue to the East River Drive, and a standing joke in my office was that you needed to keep a supply of quarters in your car not to feed parking meters but to give out to the gangs that seemed to appear in front of your car at every red light. I once parked my car at night on East 35th Street (at the time I was working in the Empire State Building) and when I came back to the vehicle I observed two gangs fighting with each other over which gang was going to break into my car.

Much of this crime wave in New York and other large cities was confined to ghetto neighborhoods, a function of the collapse of many urban economies in the 1970s along with the ravages of crack cocaine. But enough of it spilled over into middle-class neighborhoods to create a sense of fear and threat which the media then promoted because that's what the news media exists to do. But what really implanted the crime issue in everyone's mind was the 1992 Los Angeles riot which, for the first time, was a news event captured immediately as it was happening thanks to video and cable tv. By 1990, a majority of American households subscribed to at least one, if not multiple cable networks, and for the first time a phenomenon known as the '24-hour news cycle' began to influence and ultimately dominate what people watched and how they formed opinions about what they saw.

I recall that I saw hours of the Los Angeles riots on the cable channels that played in our house, and I will never forget a scene that took place on the first night of the riot when a cable helicopter sat 20 or 30 feet above street level while a gang of Black kids pulled a White man out of his car at a stoplight, chased him across the street and then beat him senseless, all of it captured on live video and seen by me and millions of other watchers all across the United States. I wasn't in the gun business at the time, but I can guarantee you that gun shops all over the country sold out all their guns the next day. And it was exactly in the years just before and after the Los Angeles riot that concealed-carry laws spread from state to state. By 1994 there were more shall-issue than may-issue states, and by 1997 shall-issue states outnumbered may-issue states by two to one.

The irony about this growth in CCW at the state level was that it went largely unnoticed because the great gun-control battles were being fought in Washington over the two gun-control bills of the Clinton administration known as Brady and the Assault Weapons Ban. As I said in the previous chapter, the Brady bill marked the first time that the Federal Government began playing an active role in determining who could own guns, while the Assault Weapons Ban marked the first time that Big Brother could determine what kinds of guns law-abiding Americans could own. Both laws represented compromises that the NRA worked feverishly to achieve. In the case of Brady, the creation of an instant, point-of-sale background check managed by the FBI replaced what had originally been an effort to legislate a national waiting-period for anyone who wanted to purchase a gun. As for the Assault Weapons Ban, its opponents were able not only to grandfather in most of the guns that were now prohibited from being sold, but also made the entire law temporary with an expiration date set at ten years after it began.

Meanwhile, with all of the hullabaloo going on in DC regarding these laws, Alaska, Arizona, Tennessee and Virginia all shifted from *may* to *shall* in 1994 alone, and five more states moved over in 1995. Most of these states patterned their new concealed-carry laws on the Florida legislation, and the NRA found it easy to identify and engage willing legislators in state after state because, after all, who didn't want to be known as the politician who stood up against crime? Meanwhile, what the Clinton bills represented to the

NRA was an unprecedented attempt *for the very first time* to actually ban guns. Which meant that the nightmare of all nightmares was finally coming true, namely, that gun control was really an effort to get rid of all guns. So promoting concealed-carry at the state level was not only a response to fears about crime, but also was an antidote to calm concerns that the Feds were going to take all the guns away. In fact, it was a brilliant strategy on the part of the NRA, and while there may or may not have been any reality behind the notion that armed citizens could make a difference in terms of protecting all of us from crime, the bottom line is that the strategy worked and worked very well.

The strategy to pass CCW laws in various states worked so well, in fact, that by 1998 the NRA found a sponsor on Capitol Hill to promote a national concealed-carry law that would work just like drivers' licenses work; i.e., good in one state, good in all states. The original sponsor was Larry Craig, Senator from Idaho whom you may recall ultimately resigned his Senate seat (actually he served out his term and didn't run for re-election) after he was arrested in a St. Paul airport bathroom in 2007, groping under the toilet stall for what he claimed was his wallet, or his car keys, but what the undercover officer who arrested him claimed was actually the officer's leg. In happier times, Craig was not only the foremost promoter of gun rights in the Senate, but was also a member of the NRA Board, a position he relinquished before he gave up his seat in the Upper House.

The bill to create a national, reciprocal CCW license had no chance of succeeding if only because of the degree to which state gun licensing requirements differed so greatly from one state to another that it would be impossible to assume that one size could fit all, particularly since even shall-issue gun states imposed more requirements for CCW than they imposed for just owning guns. In fact, many states to this day do not impose a specific licensing process for gun ownership because, thanks to Brady, the initial purchase of any firearm requires that the buyer not be disqualified because of a felony conviction, status as a fugitive, etc. And even though a few states have now allowed what is referred to as "constitutional carry;" i.e., if you can own a gun, you are *ipso facto* allowed to carry one without further licensing requirements, even the most pro-gun states (read: Florida) still impose a licensing process and licensing requirements for CCW. Aligning all these different state laws into some kind of national system that would make a concealed-carry license of one state valid in all states represents a daunting task.

But even if the reciprocal issue could be overcome in terms of bringing the CCW legal requirements of all states into some kind of coherent whole, there is also the issue of pre-license training, which is a much bigger can of worms and needs to be considered on its own terms. Civilian firearms training was the original mission when the NRA was founded in 1871, and while the organization was always a private, independent entity, much of its early training activities was geared towards maintaining gunmanship within the civilian population for times when military service required a quick infusion of men into uniform whose preparedness would be augmented by the fact that they already knew how to use and maintain guns.

The use of a primarily conscripted army after the Civil War didn't occur until the United States entered World War I, and the military was quickly demobilized in 1918 and did not rely on conscription again until the eve of World War II. Which meant that if there was a sudden need for military manpower, being able to shortcut the time and costs of firearms training was, at least in theory, a laudable idea. In fact, the only serious military venture between the Civil War and World War I was the Spanish-American War of 1898, which lasted only ten weeks but resulted in the call-up of nearly 200,000 men, most of whom were serving in National Guard units which gave most members some degree of familiarity with guns. Nevertheless, in 1903 Congress chartered the Civilian Marksmanship Program, which was an independent entity that could distribute surplus military rifles to local CMP shooting clubs, many of which were also tightly connected to the NRA. I was a member of such a club in 1955, and my CMP membership also allowed me to join the NRA.

I don't recall whether the safety instructions I received in my rifle club were from a specific NRA training course or not, but suffice it to say that the connection between the CMP and the NRA made the latter the predominant mover and shaker in civilian gun training activities throughout the United States. And as licensing for gun ownership spread from one locale to another, to the degree that such licensing incorporated some kind of training regimen as a prerequisite for gun ownership, the NRA training courses were usually codified into licensing statutes and procedures nationwide.

The problem with such codification, however, is that there are only a handful of states that require that someone actually applies for a license to own firearms before purchasing a gun. Outside of the gun-dry northwest states like New York, New Jersey, Connecticut and Massachusetts, most states allow residents to purchase firearms by just undergoing the NICS background check, and even fewer states require any kind of pre-licensing training to own guns. And of the states that do **require** safety training as a prerequisite for getting a gun license, the training usually consists of answering a few written questions on a form that is supplied with the other paperwork that must be filled out at the time that someone applies for a license to own a gun.[4]

The NRA claims to have roughly 100,000 certified gun trainers on the rolls of their Training Division, but it's unclear as to how many of these individuals engage in any training activities at all. Many of the trainers are actually active law enforcement officers who pick up a little extra cash by being designated as the "gun person" for their particular police unit; others become qualified to re-certify their fellow officers who are usually required to perform a brief shooting exercise each year to prove that they can, in fact, hit the broad side of a barn with their gun. Most NRA trainers are simply guys and a few gals who really enjoy guns along with being around other people who like guns. They show up at local matches, they are active in the shooting clubs near where they live, and when or if they actually do present a training course it's usually a nice shmooze with other gun folks where everyone stands around and fools with their guns. In the past several years the writer Dan Baum and the sociologist Jennifer Carlson both attended training classes as part of the research they conducted on gun owners and both discovered that the training was hardly conducive to teaching them anything serious about how to use and shoot guns.

You would think that with the spread of CCW that there would be a growth in concern about proper training insofar as gun owners were now being licensed not to own a gun but to carry one around for the purpose of using it in self-defense. And a majority of states do, in fact, require some kind of training as part of the process for getting licensed to walk around armed. But the training is rudimentary at best; it never requires anything more than a minimal proficiency test if there is any proficiency requirement at all, and many states issue CCW licenses without requiring the candidate to actually shoot a live gun. One of the more **popular** CCW training sites in Detroit, for example, charges $99 for the nine-hour class, which entitles to student to "classroom materials, lunch, snacks, free gun rental, range time" and, for an additional eighteen bucks, the purchase of 50 rounds of ammunition, although it's not clear that all fifty rounds will actually be used during the class.[6] In Florida, state law mandates that anyone applying for a concealed-weapon permit must demonstrate shooting proficiency by firing off at least one round. Following the 2008 Supreme Court decision that allowed D.C. residents to keep handguns in their homes, the D.C. Police Department posted an online safety course that is required before anyone can apply for a license to purchase a gun. The course takes about 20 minutes to view, there is no test to qualify whether or not someone actually watched the computer screen or not, and I viewed the entire test and ate breakfast, answered emails, paid a few bills and watched *Morning Joe* at the same time.

The NRA training guide currently lists 19 courses of which the two most popular courses, *Basic Pistol* and *Range Safety Officer Course* were designed at least fifty years ago and much of the nomenclature and graphics in the student course guides are right out of the Eisenhower years. Most shooting clubs can only get insurance coverage if they have a safety officer either on the premises or on call, so the Range Safety Officer course is taught frequently and draws a fairly steady enrollment in areas where shooting clubs and ranges are found. The *Basic Pistol* course was often required in order to become a member of a shooting range or shooting club, and it is the primary training course that is listed by those states which require any sort of training in order to qualify to walk around with a gun.

Back around 2000 the NRA updated its training materials to reflect the shift away from gun ownership to carrying a gun and produced to courses, *Personal Protection in the Home* (PPH) *and Personal Protection Outside the Home (*PPOH*)* which focus on using handguns not for shooting at a range or in a match, but for personal defense. The courses are taken in sequence, with PPH intended to be a prerequisite for PPOH, although the decision as to whether one actually needs to take PPH in order to qualify for admission to PPOH is, shall we say, a matter of choice. Prospective students are informed by the NRA Training Division that over eight hours they will learn " basic defensive shooting skills, strategies for home safety and responding to a violent confrontation, firearms and the law, how to choose a handgun for self-defense, and continued opportunities for skill development," and should be prepared to shoot 100 rounds.

Before I move into the specifics of the course, however, I want to spend a bit of time to explain how people become certified to teach this or any other NRA course. Basically, the certification process is very simple; one takes a student-level course in a particular subject area and then one takes the same course at the instructor level which means going through the same material twice, once as a student, the second time as a prospective instructor which means spending a certain amount of time reading to the other instructor candidates from the instructor, as opposed to the student manual. At the end of both classes, the student or the instructor candidate takes a brief, true-false and multiple-choice exam.

I hold six NRA instructor certifications, including *Basic Pistol* and both *Personal Protection in the Home* and *Personal Protection Outside the Home*. I enjoyed all the training sessions immensely, most of the classes were filled with gun nuts just like myself and I was lucky because I took all my certification classes from one of the best, most experienced and most likable NRA training counselors around. Let me tell you something about a well-run NRA course; you get in a room for eight hours with a bunch of other gunnies, you spend the whole day talking about guns and in some courses you even get to shoot some rounds at the range, and during those eight hours the outside world simply disappears.

On the other hand, I have to admit that in terms of actually preparing anyone to use a handgun for personal defense, these courses were a joke. The only reason that the NRA insists that the instructors slavishly follow the curriculum word-for-word is that they want to impose a certain amount of uniformity over the training activities which bear their name because, in fact, they don't impose any sort of qualification on the skills or aptitudes of the trainers themselves. Show up, pay the course fee, sit there for six or seven hours, take a simple test at the end which everyone passes and – voila! – you are certified to teach others how to defend themselves with a gun.

Back in the 1990s I saw where the future was going and decided to move myself career-wise from financial services into IT. I had been a broker for several major firms, went so far as to open my own, small financial consulting shop in New York, but then the Bush I recession which brought about the election of Clinton ("it's the economy, stupid") wiped me out. By 1995 you couldn't walk into any corporate office without seeing a PC on nearly every desk, so I put two and two together and decided to get certified as a network engineer by taking courses offered by a network software company called *Novell*.

Over a period of four months I took eight courses in sequence at a *Novell* lab, passed each course at the instructor level, and then at the end took a tough exam which certified me as being able to both administer a Novell network but also to teach networking to students who, like myself, wanted to develop a career in IT. But in addition to passing all the course exams in terms of content, I also had to appear at a different *Novell* location and demonstrate my ability to teach networking to a group of students while my performance was electronically graded by a group of unseen network engineers. And while I actually passed this test on my first shot, I met two other candidates who were trying to pass the teaching proficiency test for the third and fourth times. In other words, if you wanted to be certified in a discipline that would lead to a serious career, this wasn't the time, pardon my French, to f--k around. On the other hand, want to get certified in an activity that's just a lot of fun? Try the NRA.

But when you stop and think about it, certifying someone who then can determine whether someone else can walk around with a lethal weapon in their pocket shouldn't be so much fun. It should be a serious enterprise, as well as a weeding-out process, in order to try and find reasons why certain individuals, even if they meet the legal requirements, still shouldn't be allowed to walk around with a gun. When I teach the handgun safety course in my state I have students, usually women, who when they shoot off their first round, drop the gun and burst into tears. I know they won't ever do any serious practice or self-training; I know that if God forbid they actually picked up a gun to defend themselves it would probably be the first time they held the gun since they purchased in somebody's shop. But I can't disqualify such individuals from getting their CCW because in my state live-fire is not required as part of the safety course at all. I make everyone fire a gun because I want everyone to see, hear and feel the fact that once you pull the trigger, you can't take it back. But that's a learning *experience*, not a learning *requirement* for the legal right to carry around a gun.

And what are the actual learning requirements in my state for getting your CCW application approved? You have to take one of 6 NRA courses, your choice, that the State Police Licensing Division believes contains the necessary information for you to own and shoot a gun in a safe way. So here's an example of what you are required to learn in one of those courses, in this case *Personal Protection in the Home* which I have chosen to discuss because it was developed specifically in response to the NRA's decision to promote CCW and the armed citizen as the reasons for buying and owning guns.

The course consists of seven lessons, beginning with what is called an *Introduction to Defensive Shooting*. This lesson, which is supposed to take an hour, begins with an explanation about using a firearm "responsibly and ethically" for personal protection; developing the proper mindset for using a gun in a life-threatening situation; understanding and appreciating what the NRA calls the "four levels of awareness;" and knowing the importance of mental and physical preparation for dealing with a "life-threatening confrontation." The course also contains a chapter which is only supposed to be taught either by an attorney with specialized knowledge in the legal issues that might arise if someone used a gun in self-defense, or taught by a non-attorney with some kind of "certified" knowledge and/or experience in talking about the legal issues involved.

I took this course from a certified NRA trainer who claimed that he wasn't an attorney but that he had appeared as an expert witness in legal cases involving self-defense with a gun. I didn't hear a single thing in his presentation that was necessarily contrary to what would be considered standard operating procedure for anyone whose behavior had caused physical injury to someone else, namely, to stick around until the cops showed up, say as little as possible to anyone about anything related to the event, and make sure to connect with competent legal representation as soon as possible after the event. The syllabus clearly states that armed defense should be considered a "last resort," but it really doesn't go into any details at all about other defense options that might be employed instead of a gun. And as I am going to explain in Chapter 3, using a gun to defend yourself against a violent attack is hardly the only option, and it's not clear that it's an option that necessarily works.

The course also doesn't really explain, in legal or non-legal terms, how one would define an actual threat. At some point in the introductory lesson, the instructor is required to list various situations that might be considered a potential threat around the home. This includes an approaching stranger, an unidentified noise, a person who comes to the door asking for assistance or to use your phone and, most common, "anyone you do not know, regardless of what or who he or she claims to be." It's hard to read through this chapter, or listen to it in a class, without getting the distinct impression that anything short of continued awareness at the highest level leaves the average homeowner vulnerable to a serious attack. But nowhere in this or any other part of the course are the students made aware of the fact that: a) the odds of a home invasion which ends in violence is exceedingly rare, and, b) a majority of home invasions, even those that end in some kind of violent altercation, involve perpetrators and victims who knew each other before the event actually occurred. The whole point of this lesson and this entire course is not so much to teach defensive shooting skills, if only because shooting 100 rounds or so over the course of a couple of hours doesn't really prepare someone for any real use of a gun at all. The real point is to drive home the message that everyone is possibly the target of a serious, violent crime, a.k.a. a "threat," and the best way to respond to this environment is to have access to a gun.

The course also contains a chapter on making your home secure from an invasion both inside and out. For the latter, this involves planting trees and shrubbery that "provide cover from observation for a criminal," planting thorny bushes "to deter their use as cover," avoid living in a house that has recessed entryways and "other natural hiding places," and keeping outside lighting "well maintained." The home should have "quality, steel doors," a monitored security system and doors should, of course, be locked at all times. Nowhere in the entire course, incidentally, is any attention paid to security measures that should be developed if you happen to live in an apartment, even though most inner-city residents for whom the gun industry believes are particularly vulnerable to crime and, hence, are in the greatest need of having access to personal protection, happen to live a residence which is something other than a private home.

But leaving that issue aside, the chapter on securing the home moves from outside to inside the dwelling, and recommends that every residence contain a "safe room," which would be the one place within the home to which everyone could retreat and, when secured properly, would not allow entry by anyone except authorized personnel. The safe room should only have one entrance with an exceptionally-strong door, it should have windows with which to communicate with police or other first responders who would be contacted by using the telephone that would be standard safe equipment, and these and other features would allow everyone to "maintain a defensive posture" until help arrives on the scene.

The notion of creating safe room to which, incidentally, everyone should regularly practice entering at night with all interior lights extinguished, simply overlooks the most basic issue in self-defense, namely, the primary goal which anyone being threatened should always first consider, which is to flee. There is no other response to a threat of injury that is as effective as leaving the scene, and while one can argue that this response becomes problematic if the household being threatened contains multiple occupants, Department of Justice data confirms the fact that twice as many households where burglaries occur are occupied by a single man or woman than by multiple family members at the time the invasion occurs. This course makes no mention anywhere about exercising the option of running away, and its advice regarding how to respond to a threat inside the home flies directly in the face of what law enforcement data actually shows.

Basically the NRA approach to personal defense is a mish-mash of stand your ground, castle doctrines and responding to a threat with a gun. I'll talk about castle doctrines and stand your ground below, but suffice it to say that these self-defense philosophies gained credence and legislative legitimacy at the same time that CCW became a mainstream state of affairs. Together, they provide the legal environment in which the myth of the armed citizen flourished and grew. Taken together, they have about as much relationship to the reality of crime protection as the veritable man in the moon.

The first Stand Your Ground law was passed – where else? – in Florida in 2005. It was largely the work of Grandma Hammer who, as you may recall, was the past NRA President who got Florida to enact its CCW law in 1987. Stand Your Ground was basically an effort, now law in more than 30 states, to take the more traditional Castle Doctrine notion and move it from inside a dwelling out into the street. The Castle Doctrine – a home is a man's castle – comes from British Common Law, which was brought over and spread throughout the colonies, even though interestingly enough it is not mentioned in the Constitution or the Bill of Rights. Nevertheless, various forms of Castle Doctrine laws exist in most states and basically it allows someone to use force up to lethal force against someone who invades their home.

Note that Castle Doctrine laws do not usually require that the person who is protecting himself from an intruder prove that his assailant was actually invading his home in order to harm him or even to necessarily commit a crime. Laws covering justifiable homicide, for example, usually hold the person who does the killing to a much higher standard of proof than absent the use of lethal force the victim would have attacked and seriously injured or killed the person who then defended himself by using lethal force. In the case of most Castle Doctrine laws, however, the standard of proof required to immunize the person who uses lethal force to defend himself is much lower if there is any standard at all. The simple fact that someone enters your home against your will and refuses to leave is proof enough that your well-being is being threatened to the degree that you can and should respond with lethal force.

Stand Your Ground laws take the philosophy of Castle Doctrine and apply it to situations that could arise not in one's residence or home (many Castle Doctrines also apply to a vehicle) but anywhere that two people come into conflict and one person decides that using lethal force is required because otherwise he might face a threat of serious harm. It's understandable, perhaps, that an individual in their home should not have to vacate the premises of their residence if someone attempts to force their way in or otherwise attempt to physically invade a home. But in the case of Stand Your Ground, the idea that a simple disagreement or argument could turn into a life-ending episode just because one or the other party believes that they are facing the possibility of a lethal attack, is stretching the notion of self-defense to a radical extreme. Nevertheless, the NRA has vigorously championed Stand Your Ground laws for obvious reasons, particularly since states that open up CCW also tend to be the states where Stand Your Ground philosophies are most quickly turned into laws.

Which takes us directly to the next issue for understanding the myth of self defense, namely, if we can walk around in the street with a gun and if we can pull it out just because we believe that someone coming towards us represents a lethal threat, what are the odds that something along those lines is actually going to occur?

CHAPTER 3

PROGENITORS OF THE MYTH

The NRA's approach to defending hearth and home with a gun is intended, first of all, to create the impression that threats to one's personal wellbeing are common enough not only to justify making one's residence attack-proof, but also to maximize the best way to respond to such an attack, namely, by owning a gun. But the question which remains to be answered is this: How serious is the threat to one's personal wellbeing, and is this threat serious enough to justify owning personal-defense guns? There have always been times, of course, when gun owners used their weapons for self defense. But yanking a hunting shotgun off the wall and warning someone that you are armed is very different from going into a gun shop and asking the shop owner which kind of handgun you should buy to carry and use for personal defense. The former simply represents an expedient response to a specific situation for which having a gun around the house happened to work out for the best. The latter, on the other hand, represents a calculated decision about buying and using a gun for one thing and one thing only, namely a threat to one's personal welfare or the welfare of family and friends. The NRA's *Personal Safety in the Home* makes absolutely no effort to quantify the notion of threat at all; it simply assumes that someone is taking this course because they believe the threat to be real.

To my knowledge, the best data on how much we really have to fear from personal attacks and threats was compiled and published in 2010 by the Bureau of Justice Statistics which covered all household burglaries between 2003 and 2007.[1] And while this data might appear to be from as long as twelve years ago, the good news is that burglary rates have actually fallen slightly from those years, so what was valid for understanding home threats back then is probably just as valid now.

The BJS data is as follows. Of the average 3,700,000 burglaries committed annually between 2003 and 2007, someone was in the home 27% of the time and 7% were victims of violence by the perpetrator. In other words, somewhere between one million and 260,000 Americans might have found themselves in situations in which they needed to defend themselves from bodily harm. I tend to suspect that the actual number of people who might have been in a position that required them to consider using lethal force to defend themselves in their homes was probably closer to the lower figure, not because I am trying to dismiss or denigrate the argument for the use of deadly force, but because the BJS report points out that of burglaries where someone was present at the time of the incident, almost half took place because the offender was either let into the residence by someone inside, or the offender had a key. The likelihood that a majority of home invasions take place without any degree of surprise is also borne out by the fact that the offender and the person present in the home knew each other prior to the incident taking place.

Note that the NRA training on home defense doesn't mention that the victim might know the attacker as a possible scenario at all. The training manual advises students to always maintain a high level of awareness because the threat might come from a stranger, or by someone coming to the front door and asking for help, or perhaps you might hear a strange noise. But according to the BJS report, there's a good chance that the person who tries to gain entrance to your home for the purpose of robbing and/or injuring you is someone who has been in your home before. And it's probably someone you know.

I was sitting in my gun shop several weeks ago when a letter arrived from another retail dealer whose store is located about forty miles away. The dealer is also named Mike, he's a nice, older guy, and if he didn't have to open the shop every day he'd be stuck at home with "the wife." I'd be stuck at home with "the cat" which basically amounts to the same thing. Anyway, the purpose of this letter was to advise me and every other dealer in our area that one of his customers had just lost 30 or so guns that were stolen out of his home. Attached to the letter was a list of the guns – make, model, serial number, the usual stuff. The letter went on to ask me to be on the lookout if anyone tried to come into my shop and sell me some of these guns. If that actually happened, I should call a certain cop in his town who had been assigned the case.

I was somewhat jealous as I read the list because, to be honest, there were a few guns that had been stolen from this poor guy which I would have liked to own. This included a couple of Colt .45 pistols, you never have enough Colts (right now I only have three), a Ruger Mini-30, a couple of medium-grade Winchester Model 70 rifles, all together a very nice list. I happened to be working on this manuscript when the letter arrived so I immediately picked up the phone and called the gun dealer, Mike, to get some more details about the theft. And in answer to my "how did it happen" question, he said, "It was your standard smash and grab, the cops think it was an inside job."

Notice the words, "an inside job." That house was invaded and those guns were stolen by someone who had been in that house previously and knew the guns were there. Maybe it was someone who even lived in the house or the friend of a friend. I had two Browning handguns stolen from my house because one weekend my wife and I went away and told her daughter that she could stay in the house with her good-for-nothing boyfriend whom she later had the good sense to finally dump. But at some point during that weekend they also went off the property during which time an even more worthless friend of the boyfriend showed up and boosted the two guns. How do I know who stole the guns? Because the strong box in which I kept the guns was later found in the back yard of the apartment house where the good-for-nothing's worse-for-nothing's friend happened to live.

I'm not saying there's no chance that someone's residence won't be invaded and their lives put at risk. It happens all the time. But recently a Federal court in California heard and rejected an appeal from some gun owners who were challenging San Francisco's municipal ordinance which requires that all guns be locked or otherwise mechanically disabled in order to be stored in the home.[2] And one of the plaintiffs challenging the law was an elderly woman, claiming to be "older than seventy-nine" who said that if she heard a strange noise, first she had to turn on the light, then she had to put on her glasses, then she had to walk across the room to where she kept her guns locked away, then she had to fumble for the key, then he had to unlock the gun. By the time she got done with all this rigmarole, she knew that her attacker would have plenty of time to assault her, rob her home and leave her for dead.

What she didn't say to the Court was that the odds of such a sequence of events actually taking place wasn't the same as the odds that she would go outside and get run over by a rhinoceros; the odds were about the same that she would go outside and get attacked by someone who had just landed from Mars. As it turns out, the Court was unmoved by this madcap recitation of what would happen to the little old lady who wasn't allowed to just reach under the pillow and pull out a gun. The bottom line of the BJS report on forcible entries is that, generally speaking, maybe at best a quarter of a million Americans each year, and maybe only half that many, actually experience the fright and abject terror of suddenly finding themselves facing an unknown intruder who may or may not be bent on doing them harm. But that's hardly the impression conveyed by the NRA's Introductory lesson on home defense which emphasizes the importance of remaining "alert to your environment," and if there's any doubt about what this really means, the NRA recommends that everyone should base their awareness of this issue on the four or five-step tactical awareness training developed and employed by the military every day.

So why do Americans feel that the only way they can effectively respond to threats against their well-being is to own and carry a gun? First of all, let's be clear on the point that when I say that "Americans" feel they need to carry a gun for self-defense, I am not talking about a majority of Americans. In fact, on a proportional and even numerical basis, the number of Americans who own guns keeps going down.

This is a very important point to bear in mind because at the same time that CCW is now legally mandated in one form or another by all 50 states, the spread in concealed-carry laws and the increase in the issuance of concealed-carry has not been matched by an increase in the number of people who own guns. The General Social Survey has been tracking gun ownership from the 1970s, when more than half the households represented in the survey reported that they owned at least one gun. The percentage of gun-owning households fell into the forty percent range by the 1980s, remained there or went slightly lower in the 1990s, and then dipped into the thirty percentile after 2000. The only thing which keeps the overall percentage above 30% is the fact that more than 50% of those families identifying themselves as Republicans also own guns; among Democrat and Independent households gun ownership is down to one out of four.

Some of the pro-gun advocates try to dampen the enthusiasm of the gun-control community about these numbers by pointing out that the percentage decline in gun ownership, if true, is not that significant because the U.S. population has grown nearly 50% between 1975 and 2015, from roughly 215 million to 315 million over those forty years. But there's really little comfort to be taken from that argument for the following reasons.

First, if 50% of the 1975 population meant that approximately 107 million people were members of families that owned guns, 32% of the 2015 population means that the total numeric for gun owners now stands at 100 million, give or take a million here or there. In fact the proportional decline of gun ownership is pronounced to the point that the absolute number has also slightly declined, and just imagine how high it would be (roughly 150 million rather than 100 million) if the 50% of the country that were gun owners in 1975 were still gun owners today.

Another, even more disquieting bit of news about gun ownership comes not from the General Social Survey but from Pew's polling on the attitudes of millennials who, by and large, appear to differ sharply from older generations when it comes to the issue of guns.[3] To sum it up, they're basically not terribly interested in becoming gun owners, and this is also true of other, non-white male demographics like women, new immigrants, Hispanics and Blacks. Insofar as these groups are fast becoming the motors for demographic growth in the country as a whole, the downward slide of gun ownership that the GSS reported in its latest survey may be a harbinger of even greater declines in guns and gun ownership for the years ahead.

For the gun industry what these poll numbers suggest is the need to redouble their efforts to keep their current ownership base as interested as possible in buying more guns. And here is the great irony in all of this, namely, the success of the gun lobby in promoting the notion of guns as mainstream products from a political point of view hasn't necessarily resulted in a growth in gun ownership. Quite to the contrary, the fact that it is legally much easier to acquire and use guns than previously may, in fact, have a dampening effect on gun ownership overall.

The reason I say that is because, like it or not, the gun industry has only found its products to be in high demand when people who own guns feel that they might lose their guns or encounter additional legal difficulties in acquiring guns. You might think, for example, that in an age of terrorism more average people would begin to think about guns for self-defense if for no other reason than a generalized fear that government can no longer protect us against threats. But this has not been the case. True, there was a slight spike in gun sales after 9-11, but by the time this market spike was noticed by the popular press it was over and done. The administration of George W. Bush may have seen an extension of legal protections for the gun industry, but it sure didn't result in manna falling from heaven for the local gun shop down the street. In the run-up to the 2012 election, when Republicans were selling themselves on the idea that no sitting President could get re-elected with unemployment in double digits, retailers couldn't give guns away because everyone was convinced that the Obama "threat" to gun ownership was about to go away.

The myth of the armed citizen may have been a brilliant marketing scheme on the part of the gun industry to at least keep gun sales on a par with where they had been for previous generations when hunting drove the gun industry both in terms of product design and sales. But if the industry was going to promote this myth for gun ownership it also needed new types of products and some mythmakers who could develop and spread the myth itself. Let's look first at the products which the gun industry developed to help consumers begin thinking about self-defense.

Which means we have to start with Gaston Glock. I was living in New York City when the first Glock pistols began to show up in 1984 or 1985. Every three months there was a gun show up the Hudson River at Kingston, and a bunch of us would drive up from "da city" to attend the show. There were 4 or 5 of us, all confirmed gun nuts and, for the most part, cops. Which means we could "buy on shield," as the saying went, without doing any paperwork at all. Actually, the fact that we had police identification didn't mean we were exempt from filling out 4473s, but remember that this was pre-Brady days, so even FFL-dealers who sold at gun shows didn't really care. And for the most part the ATF guys walking around the show were only there to look for automatic weapons and the local cops were mostly gun nuts themselves. So if you walked around with some cash you could pretty much buy anything that was for sale. Ahh, the good old days.

The first time I saw a Glock was at a Kingston show when I ended up buying the same gun twice. I was wandering around at the show and found a guy who wanted to sell his Smith & Wesson Model 58, which was the 4-inch, 41-magnum revolver with combat sights. He wanted 400 bucks for the gun, I offered 350, and a few seconds later for 375 I owned this beautiful piece of hardened steel. Maybe I walked another 50 feet, maybe less when one of my guys, Jackie Clark, came up to me, saw the 58 in my hand and yelled out, "I gotta have that gun!" Now it happened that I owed Jackie a favor because a few weeks earlier he had given me his black leather NYPD jacket with the gold buttons which was my daughter's favorite outfit and, when she wore it, made her the most popular kid in her 7th-grade class. And Jackie had basically given me the jacket for free when other cops were selling their jackets for a hundred bucks or more. The NYPD had switched from leather to velour, now they looked like every other police department in the United States and the leather jackets (made out of beautiful French leather) commanded a nice price.

So I gave the Model 58 to Jackie right there in the middle of the show and I walked off down one aisle and he went off to look at guns on the other side of the hall. Half an hour later we bumped into each other again and the Model 58 was gone and in its place was this ugly piece of black plastic which Jackie told me was a 9mm pistol known as a Glock. Jackie had heard about the gun; he was for sure the biggest gun nut among all of us so he would have known about this gun before it became common parlance among the cops. As much as he wanted that Model 58, what he really wanted was to be the first cop in the one-two-oh precinct, if not in the entire City of New York to own a Glock. So I ran back to the dealer who had traded the Glock to Jackie for his Model 58; the Smith was still sitting on his table, I gave him the 400 bucks and the 41-magnum revolver was mine once again.

Just to bring this story full circle I should tell you that about a year later I traded the Model 58 to a guy I met at another gun show who worked as an armorer at Colt's, when the company was then located on Huyshope Avenue alongside the Connecticut River and was still in the original factory building with the gold, rampant colt atop the old dome. Anyway, this guy, whose name I didn't even know, got the Model 58, and in return he took my Colt AR-15 that I was toting around the show, went out to his car and then returned a few minutes later having installed a full-auto sear which, he assured me, made the gun a real machine gun that was "up to factory specs." The full-auto AR ended up paying for some Mikuni carbs that I later put on my Harley Low Rider, but back to the Glock.

So we all left the gun show in Kingston and drove to New York. The following week Jackie took his new Glock up to the licensing division so that the illustrious Mrs. Skiba could list the gun in Jackie's file, and that's when all hell broke loose. Because even though Jackie was a cop, in fact a member of the borough SWAT team, every gun that was acquired under a personal license in New York City not only had to be registered by Mrs Skiba and Jose, but also had to be inspected by one of the cops who had somehow got themselves assigned to the licensing division, which was a far better detail than patrolling some goddamn Harlem street. And the licensing division initially rejected the *Glock* and told Jackie that he couldn't own the gun because it was made out of plastic and therefore wouldn't set off alarms if Jackie attempted to walk through a metal detector at the Supreme Court building on Centre Street with the Glock under his arm. Six months later, after not one but two trips to the NYPD pistol range at Rodman's Neck, Jackie finally convinced the NYPD brass that his *Glock* would, in fact, set off a metal detector because the barrel, by the way, would only handle real ammunition if it was made out of steel.

That was 1983 or 1984. By 1994, if you were a cop just about anywhere in the United States, you weren't carrying a *Smith&Wesson* any more, you were carrying a *Glock*. And the reason you were carrying a *Glock* was because the Glock held 15 or 16 rounds of ammunition while a revolver held only 6 rounds, the *Glock* usually worked even after it was dropped from a six-story window and, best of all, the gun never rusted and really didn't need to be cleaned. And the last thing any cop wants to do when he finishes his shift is to sit down and clean the friggin' gun. That's what polymer is all about. It's lightweight, strong as hell and doesn't rust. Finally, the way the gun was designed, you could also attach a light or a laser to the frame and thus illuminate the target area without having to take one hand off the gun.

The *Glock* had other engineering and design changes that went beyond the polymer finish, chief of which had to do with the actual manufacturing process that produced the gun. Because the good news about polymer was that the entire frame of the gun could be cut and shaped out of a cast that would create the exact, same-sized frame every time, and then all you had to do was drop a trigger assembly into the frame – *thwack* – bang it into place with a holding screw, then drop a hammer assembly into the slide – *thwack* – bang it into place with a holding screw and – *viola!* – the gun is done. No more endless fitting and polishing of internal parts, no more applying an acid-based finish and then polishing some more. When I walked around the *Smith & Wesson* factory in 1981 it was basically a bunch of highly-skilled craftsmen operating under one roof and building one gun at a time. Take a tour of that same factory today – the guns are all made with cad-cam machines, no live hands touch them at all, and they tumble out a dozen every time the finishing plate on the cad-cam machine whirrs around.

To the gun industry, polymer meant durability, cheap manufacture, lightweight and small size. *Glock* began bringing handguns to the market that were 6 inches long and weighed less than one pound. *Smith & Wesson* had an aluminum-frame revolver which weighed about the same but held only 5 rounds while the *Glock* pistol was a ten-shot deal. Remember that the1990s was also the time when small started to become better and consumers would pay more for miniaturization and portability (laptops versus desktops) even if this meant sacrificing some of the features and performance that larger models usually employed. The only thing that consumers gave up when going from a full-size to a concealable handgun was the ability to use a longer barrel to sight the target. But this didn't matter because at close-quarters, which is what armed self-defense is all about, you didn't need to aim the gun anyway. Just point and fire, and if the gun is equipped with a laser, then no aim is really required at all.

The polymerization of long guns was what brought the AR-style rifle, from a marketing perspective, into full bloom. A standard AR with a collapsible stock (thanks to polymer) is less than 3 feet in length and weighs 7 pounds. The M1 Garand is nearly 4 feet long and weighs between 9.5 and 11 pounds. The AR can take all kinds of doodads like "tactical" rails, lights, lasers, sight systems and so on and so forth. The M1 Garand cannot be "personalized" at all. *Stag Arms*, which makes what is probably the best AR on the market today, is advertising the Executive Survivor Kit, which consists of an AR rifle packed into a Pelican carrying case, and along with the rifle you get a cleaning kit, a Gerber flashlight and Gerber multi-pliers, some ammunition, a "dual purpose" human/animal first aid kit and a MRE field ration kit.

I want to stop here for a minute and talk about MREs or what is called Meals Ready to Eat. You can find this stuff all over the internet; it's basically army surplus or stuff that pretends to be army surplus and, as one purveyor of this crap advertises, it is "designed for maximum endurance and nutrition with average 1250 calories per meal." Now let's go back to the Stag Executive Survivor Kit which, by the way, retails for 2,000 bucks. Can you imagine that there's the faintest possibility that someone, anyone in the United States would ever really need a survivor kit unless he was trying to avoid being audited by the IRS? I was audited by the IRS last year, the audit dragged on for month after month, and there were times that I actually day-dreamed about sneaking away from home, driving for a week to get to Alaska, and then hiding out until both my wife and the IRS thought I was dead. But knowing me, by the third night that I was out trying to "survive" in the bush I would probably check into the nearest Holiday Inn. Get it? What Stag Arms is appealing to with its Executive Survivor Kit are the same people who go off to Thunder Ranch and ante up a couple of thousand bucks to play *Terminator 3* with a live gun.

But the fact is that a lot of people out there who really and truly believe that they need to be prepared to defend themselves with a gun, and the myth is based partially on the products and the product marketing that has characterized the gun industry since polymer and digital optics became available both for guns and other consumer items. But the self-defense myth was also a function of the energies and talents of a group of myth-makers who began talking and promoting armed defense well before the industry realized where the market was headed and began producing products that promoted self-defense as well.

If there is one person to whom the we owe the development and propagation of the self-defense myth it is Jeff Cooper, whose writings on guns, gun culture and gun use represents a remarkable bibliography unmatched by anyone else in the entire universe of guns. In many respects, whether he knew it or not, Cooper was a latter-day Theodore Roosevelt, combining a passionate love of the outdoors with hunting and a veneration of the American "spirit" as exemplified through gun ownership, self-protection and 2nd-Amendment rights. In his latter years, Cooper attracted the usual assortment of gun-loving, New Right characters like G. Gordon Liddy and Oliver North, but his political panderings, while not unusual for pro-gun personalities, always took a back seat to his writings and promotion about guns.

Cooper's classic work, which really created the whole discussion of using guns for personal defense, was entitled *Principles of Personal Defense* and was first published in 1972. What nobody seems to have ever noticed is that the portrait of Cooper by Paul Kirchner, shows Cooper with a military-style safari cap that appears to have a remarkable likeness to a Luftwaffe flying eagle logo which, given Kirchner's personalized approach to illustrations, might not be as far-fetched as one might think. Be that as it may, the very first words of the book set the tone and approach for the entire self-defense myth: "Some people prey on other people. Whether we like it or not, this is one of the facts of life."

Cooper then goes on to attach his response to this "fact of life" with the following: "The author assumes that the right of self-defense exists." So now we have the *fact* of human aggression mitigated by the Biblically-inspired notion of self-defense. Which doesn't yet get us to the complete myth but we're almost there. Because in order to complete the myth, we have to bring in the existence of a gun. And Cooper does that by noting another *fact*, namely, that most people are "simply unprepared for the fact of human savagery." And in order to be prepared, one must follow certain principles of preparedness at any and all times, which requires one to be alert, decisive, aggressive, speedy, cool, ruthless and always thinking in terms of surprising the adversary before he can surprise you.

As I read through Cooper's text, my regret is that he didn't live into the digital age, because much of the commentary in *Principles of Personal Defense* reads like the script for a video game. Come to think of it, the tactics he espouses usually form the movement and scenarios for best-selling video games like *Call of Duty: Black Ops* or *Modern Warfare* whose players normally range in age from twelve to fifteen. In fact, I'll point this out now and come back to it later on, what I find impressive about Cooper's style in a perverse way is that it really appears to have been written for readers who have not yet lived beyond their teen-age years. Because what it evokes on virtually every page is a predator-like world in which danger and threats lurk at every turn.

But the video game industry is not the only place where Cooper's version of modern life and its threats appear. In fact, his advice on how to identify and respond to threats has also been incorporated into the training curriculum of the NRA. Cooper is best known for the development of what he referred to as an "awareness code," which referred to how an individual would assess his surroundings in order to respond to a threat. The code was based on colors, with the lowest level of perception being white and the highest or most serious being red. The code goes like this:

White: Unaware and unprepared. Basically unable to defend against an attack.

Yellow: Relaxed but aware that a threatening situation could develop.

Orange: Something is wrong, you don't know exactly what it is, but a threat may be developing.

Red: Combat situation is in progress and time to respond.

This color code and its behavioral responses can be found in the NRA training manuals for self-defense inside and outside the home. It is used in these NRA courses to justify the idea that self-defense is not only a good thing to understand, but a necessary life strategy in order to be prepared for modern life. And most of all, it becomes the justification for carrying a gun. On that issue, Cooper also promulgated a brief list of gun safety rules which embody the idea that anyone could, at any time, be facing a serious threat:

All guns are always loaded.

Never let the muzzle cover anything you are not willing to destroy.

Keep your finger off the trigger until your sights are on the target.

Identify your target and what is behind it.

Notice here again the idea that a gun is to be used not for sporting purposes, but for confrontations with other individuals who might or might not also be carrying a gun. And this is the world that Jeff Cooper wants everyone to believe they inhabit – a world in which at any moment a serious, predatory threat might appear.

Cooper began putting his self-defense writings into practice when he opened a shooting ranch, *Gunsite*, outside of Paulden, Arizona, in 1976. The site is something akin to a dude ranch without horses but with guns, and it offers a variety of shooting experiences all packed into day-long or week-long "courses" that, one way or another, underscore the idea of self-defense. You have to bring your own guns and gear and the courses run about $300 per day. Here's how a course in pistol self-defense got started, according to a description posted by a student on the *Gunsite* blog:

> Most attacks, the instructor explained, are launched within "conversational distances" of you—a couple yards or less. The instructor had a volunteer stand in front of the class. He then backed off 21 feet, and, pretending to

have a knife in hand, rushed the volunteer. Time between his rush and touching the volunteer with his "knife" was less than two seconds. It was a sobering display. At best, a victim might be able to get a concealed-carry handgun out of its holster. Might. If the attacker was say, five feet away? No way.

The world's a dangerous place, sooner or later you'll be attacked, but what you'll learn at *Gunsite* will prepare you to deal with what Cooper called the "savagery" of human life. And just to make sure that you're prepared to deal with that savagery at every juncture of your life, you can always drop into the *Gunsite* boutique to purchase clothing, gear, jewelry, training videos and, of course, all of Cooper's books.

Cooper may have been the first gun writer to promote the idea of armed self-defense in a big way but he's certainly not the last. He's got plenty of imitators out there now, of which the best-known and most active is a writer turned armed-defense guru named Massad Ayoob, whom you might think comes from somewhere in the Near East, but in fact hails from a small town in New Hampshire where he served with the local police. Ayoob has been writing about guns since the 1980s and also peddles his self-defense bromides on CD-ROMS and online. For a number of years he promoted himself through something called the *Lethal Force Institute* but that's become a new gig known as *the Massad Ayoob Group*, a.k.a. *Threat Management for Responsible Armed Citizens.*

Ayoob hasn't yet built a gunslinging ranch or vacation spot for his courses, although he's now located in Florida so I'm sure he wouldn't have a problem finding some undeveloped swamp land which he could turn into a shooting range. In the meantime, he's taken his show on the road and gives two-day classes in various spots around the country, the courses being described as, " A two-day, 20-hour immersion course in rules of engagement for armed law-abiding private citizens, emphasizing legal issues, tactical issues, and aftermath management. Topics will include interacting with suspects, witnesses, responding police officers…threat recognition and mind-set…management of social and psychological aftermath after having had to use lethal force in defense of self or others…and preparing beforehand for legal repercussions and minimizing exposure to them. Situations in the home, at the place of business, or "on the street" will all be covered."

The courses do not involve live-fire but I'm sure that Ayoob shows up with some of his books for sale, as well as advertisements and promotional materials for various other self-defense operations who are listed on his site. When I looked at Ayoob's website I chose at random a company called *Threat Management Institute*, located in Minnesota, which claims to run self-defense courses for $400 but didn't actually have any specific courses or dates listed online. What they did have was a description of what they call the *MAG-20/ Live Fire* course, pioneered in the 1970s by Ayoob and designed to "bring out your maximum potential to accurately fire and safely manipulate a handgun when faced with the debilitating stress of a life-threatening encounter." The *Threat Management Institute* also offers a a course called *Armed Citizens' Rules of Engagement* which is allegedly taught by Ayoob himself and is considered "the national standard for the training of law abiding citizens in the use of lethal force in self defense."

Threat Managament Institute is one of 35 self-defense training operations listed on Ayoob's website, all of whom evidently teach or try to teach the Ayoob self-defense curriculum. Another listing is a company called *Derby Guns* in Scottsdale, whose website announces the cancellation of the 2014 MAG classes as well as the closing of the gun shop altogether. On the other hand, a company called *Defender Firearms Training* had classes scheduled every weekend in June and appears to be the handiwork of a former Marine corporal named Louis Arroyo, who holds eight NRA training certifications, is also certified in CPR and runs a martial arts dojo, although nowhere on the entire website are we told the address where classes will be held.

I have to give Ayoob some credit for coming up with a marketing scheme which is based on a franchise approach to teaching armed self-defense. First he created these courses which evidently have a fixed curricular content, not unlike the fixed content found in the training manuals of the NRA. Then he also certifies instructors to teach his courses and, judging from some of the testimonials of the training operations on his website, grants them a certain exclusive territory in which only one outfit can present Ayoob-developed training products in that particular place. In a way, Ayoob is trying to create an armed-defense training program similar to what the NRA offers using NRA-certified instructors and NRA-approved training plans. I wouldn't be surprised if Ayoob's courses will also start to turn up on the approved course list in states where CCW requires some kind of training experience before you can walk around with a gun.

One other myth-making entity in the world of personal defense deserves to be mentioned, and this is the Oregon-based operation known as *Thunder Ranch*. This operation is run by another self-styled gun-defense expert named Clint Smith. He came out of the Marine Corps, did some time in a police agency and then ended up working at *Gunsite* until he left to open *Thunder Ranch* in 1993. Where *Thunder Ranch* departs from *Gunsite* and other shooting schools is it emphasis on military-style shooting activities and close-combat shooting events. While students can take the usual gamut of armed-defense handgun courses, *Thunder Ranch* is known for its shotgun and AR shooting activities, its courses including *Urban Rifle*, which teaches how to "defend yourself" with a rifle and *Urban Precision Rifle*, which teaches " the surgical application of the scoped rifle to urban and compressed environments."

I love the verbiage for *Urban Precision Rifle* because it really does meet the fantasy of anyone who really wishes that he could have deployed to a terrorist zone like Somalia without actually having to do anything except show up at *Thunder Ranch*. In addition to shooting your rifle at all kinds of targets, you actually get to run through some live-fire scenarios called *Thunderville* and *Terminator 3*; I thought the latter was actually a Schwarzenegger movie, but maybe the folks who visit *Thunder Ranch* think that they're actually in a movie. Incidentally, in the previous sentence I didn't mean to imply that "run through" a scenario required the participant to actually move at any kind of quick speed. I know several gun guys who had a wonderful time at *Thunder Ranch* and I can tell you that neither of them can move from one spot to another except at a very slow pace. They're not kids, after all.

There are two other commercial manifestations of the "armed citizen" phenomenon that deserve mention. The first is a proliferation of lights, lasers and all kinds of accessories that can be mounted on long guns and handguns which are directly connected to the use of these weapon for self-defense, or what is politely known as "tactical" gun use. Until the 1980s, the inventory of a typical gun shop consisted primarily of guns, ammunition and accessories, of which the accessory category consisted overwhelmingly of cleaning kits, handgun holsters, long gun carrying cases and manually-adjustable optics for rifles. Selling a handgun often included a holster and a cleaning kit; selling a rifle often included a scope and the mounting hardware, selling either a long gun or a handgun usually meant adding on a box of ammunition or maybe two.

At best, adding 50 rounds of ammunition, a holster and a cleaning kit might add fifty or sixty bucks to the cost of a handgun; adding a scope to a rifle could add $400 or more if it was a top-of-the-line Leupold, but the optical requirements for most hunters could be met with a Burris or a cheap BSA for 100 bucks. None of these accessories added any real value to the gun and no matter how many guns I sold with or without accessories, the revenue from gun alone usually accounted for more than 80% of the total cash that ran through my store.

This degree to which accessories moved from being an after-thought to a major part of the gun dealer's revenue began to change as the industry moved from steel to polymer, began promoting the whole notion of "tactical" guns, and pushed consumers to think more about using guns for self-defense. Handgun companies like Glock overtly appealed to the notion that the only *real* reason to buy and own one of their products was to defend oneself against all kinds of dangerous threats; by post 9-11 the AR-style military rifle had become far and away the best-selling long gun design in virtually every shop.

Perhaps the most successful and innovative accessory company was and still is *Crimson Trace,* which first marketed a laser designed for handguns in 1994. The laser came pre-installed in a rubber grip which fit snugly around the stock of the handgun, replacing the factory-installed grips, and the laser itself operated either with pressure from the hand or with a switch on the side or back of the grip. Each grip came with a small Allen wrench which allowed the user to align the laser with the barrel, and the product came packaged with replacement batteries, a cute little felt storage bag and a readable instructions manual which showed you how to install and service your laser grip.

I first started to sell *Crimson Trace* products in 2002 or 2003 and what impressed me about the product line was its utter uselessness on the one hand but, at the same time, its high price. The grips sold for as much as $300 retail, which was in some cases only $100 less than the price of the gun. And since the markup on the grips was actually higher than the margin that I made on guns, what would have been a one-hundred profit from the sale of a concealable Smith & Wesson J-frame revolver now became a two-hundred dollar profit if the gun also included a *Crimson Trace*. I sold several hundred or more of these lasers every year until around 2005, and I never heard of a single consumer who ever had any reason to use the laser in a self-defense or "tactical" situation at all. But I'll deal with the issue of whether self-defense with guns has anything to do with reality when I get to Chapter 6.

I stopped selling laser and light accessories in 2005 or 2006 for the simple reason that the internet basically robbed me and every other gun retailer of what otherwise would have been a promising way to rack up some extra sales. The internet was never that much competition when it came to guns, because other than people who wanted to buy a very special, usually antique or collectible gun, the average buyer always wanted to touch and play with the gun before deciding which one was going home. Plus, most gun sales are totally impulsive and they take place because someone who likes guns walks into a gun shop, finds himself surrounded by bangers of this type or that, and just can't resist the urge to buy it and then sneak it into the basement of the house while the old lady's upstairs putting dinner on the stove.

Once self-defense products came of age on the internet, this provoked a second wave of digital marketing comprised of endless CD-ROMS that allegedly taught armed, self-defense tactics to anyone out there who was thinking or was already carrying around a gun. Perhaps the most aggressively marketed company is something called the *United States Concealed Carry Association*, which is actually a for-profit company owned by another company called *Delta Defense Network* (note the tactical reference), which would make you think that it's all about self-defense. But in fact what it's really all about is using the internet to make money through creating a membership website which basically means getting people to join a virtual organization and pay money simply to be members of something that they all think is important. The owner, a guy named Tim Schmidt, has developed a marketing approach which he calls tribal marketing, which means motivating people to "gather around something they don't like." And of course what's easier not to like then that criminal or that threat that you want to protect yourself against with a gun?

I don't know what Schmidt pays for the privilege, but the website features a personalized appeal by none other than Sean Hannity, on whose radio show Schmidt's operation runs constant ads. Once you join USCCA you get the magazine, which contains a variety of stories about concealed-carry, and of course you can also purchase a whole library of concealed-carry CD-ROMs. Schmidt claims that the average members sticks with him for 26 months, which is evidently more than twice as long as the average person sticks with any membership site. But while Schmidt's website may be the most successful and aggressive internet approach to CCW training, it's hardly the only one. In fact, even the NRA, which has always promoted the idea that gun training of any sort must be conducted face-to-face, can't resist the allure of digital revenue and has begun selling its own library of CD-ROMs.

All of these courses at *Gunsite, Thunder Ranch* and Ayoob's franchises, the tactical accessories that are often as expensive as the guns, and the books and videos which help every gun-owner develop skills in self-defense, are really nothing more than marketing strategies allowing grownups to play live-fire video games using toys that happen to be real guns. The last time that I can recall anyone using an assault rifle in a battle-like, close-quarter urban zone was when John Allen Muhammed, a.k.a. the Beltway sniper, shot and killed ten people around Washington, D.C. in October, 2002. And while the "sniper" image has become a standard bit of popular culture thanks to the unending Iraq-Afghanistan War, there's simply no chance that any non-military personnel in the United States would ever find themselves trying to take out "the enemy" at 500 yards. Or 50 yards, for that matter.

The truth is that the real reason that self-defense is a myth is because, outside of some specific demographic and geographic coordinates which I'll discuss in Chapter 6, the United States, particularly those parts of the United States inhabited by most of the people who believe they need to prepare themselves to use a gun in self-defense, happens to be a remarkably law-abiding and non-violent society where the types of physical attacks to which people might need to defend themselves rarely take place. But try telling that to the nine justices who sit on the

Supreme Court and have created the sacred text that embodies the myth of self-defense most of all. Which is what the next chapter is all about.

CHAPTER 4

THE MYTH'S SACRED TEXT

First we have the myth itself. Then we have the myth-makers. Finally we have a sacred text. And even if nobody reads the text it can be iconically referenced because this gives the myth its true meaning, its importance, is quasi-religious and thus unquestioned value as a myth.

There are three sacred texts which enshrined the armed citizen myth of which the most important was the 2008 Supreme Court decision that codified the myth into law. But before we look at that penultimate sacred document, we will spend a few pages talking about the texts which preceded the 2008 Heller decision, because it was the arguments found in those earlier texts which would then be used to construct and justify the 2008 document – District of Columbia vs. Heller – the most important armed citizen mythical text of all.

We begin first with a telephone survey published in a student law journal in 1995 which asked survey respondents to state whether they had ever used a gun to defend themselves from what they believed would have otherwise been a criminal attack against themselves or someone else. You might think that this survey was a major, ongoing effort because it was called the National Self-Defense Survey (NSDS) and its findings were compared with the findings of the National Crime Victimization Survey (NCVS) which is published every two years. The truth is that the only thing these two surveys have even remotely in common is a similar-sounding name. Try saying them both quickly or better yet, blurt out the two acronyms one after another – they sound remarkably alike.

The NCVS has been conducted since 1973 by the Bureau of Justice Statistics, an agency that collects, analyzes and publishes findings on crime for the Department of Justice. The survey is conducted on a face-to-face basis, it collects, tabulates and publishes responses from 90,000 households who are interviewed twice each year. The aggregated data represents responses from roughly 160,000 persons in those households. In addition to issuing multiple reports about each survey, the BJS also publishes the raw data and the actual questionnaires utilized in each survey.[1] When the U.S. Government says it is conducting a national survey, they mean a national survey.

The results of the National Self-Defense Survey was published one time only.[2] It was conducted by a private group of interviewers who were paid by the two criminologists who published the results. It was conducted by telephone, there was no attempt to validate the responses through additional calls or call-backs, neither the raw data nor the questionnaires were ever made publicly available and the entire national survey was based on completed interviews with 221 individuals who took the trouble to stay on the phone. This was the full extent of the survey activity that produced the National Self-Defense Survey, an exercise that was never repeated again and one which bears about as much similarity to the methods and analysis of the NVCS as the man in the moon.

But if you think the difference in methodology and analytical thoroughness was extreme between the NCVS versus the NSDS, get prepared to deal with the difference in results. And the results were as follows: The NCVS found that guns were used as a defensive measure against crime roughly 100,000 times each year. The NSDS survey, on the other hand, posited that defensive gun use (DGU) occurred more than several million times each year.

The publication of the NSDS survey provoked what I refer to in The Great American Gun

Argument as the "great DGU war," with proponents of both views holding forth in print, in online media and in many video interviews over the past twenty years. I would prefer that you read my detailed (and highly critical) analysis of this survey in Volume 4 of my series (but don't worry, you can purchase the Kindle edition for just a few bucks or get it for free if you are a Kindle subscriber) but I'll give you some headlines here.

The possibility that armed citizens were preventing several million crimes from being committed each year by making the alleged criminal aware of the fact that they were carrying a gun is remote, if not absolutely impossible for the following reasons. First, the survey respondents were never asked how they actually knew that the person against whom they brandished or actually fired a gun (the latter allegedly occurring in only 15% of the DGUs reported in the poll) were, in fact, intent or even thinking about committing a crime. They were not asked to describe what their alleged attacker said, or did, or in any other way indicated his intention as to what he planned to do. Second, while survey respondents were asked to identify themselves by race, they were not asked to identify the race of the person against whom they committed their DGU.

The failure to ask alleged DGU-committers about the race of their alleged potential assailant, as far as I am concerned, renders this entire survey worthless from any objective point of view. When law enforcement officers are trained to use lethal force, much of the training involves the need to understand and identify the times at which lethal force should be used. The fact that an individual approaches you in what you perceive to be a menacing way; the fact that someone says something to you which might sound like they might be considering a criminal act; neither of these scenarios actually means that you are facing any kind of criminal or violent threat.

These considerations become much more potent when the two individuals involved in the alleged confrontation happen to be of different racial types, in particular White and Black. We can talk all we want about how the legal landscape has changed relative to racial discrimination, and we can also congratulate ourselves on the degree to which racism in an overt, institutionalized sense has more or less gone away. But our urban housing is more segregated than ever, the degree to which Blacks and Whites co-mingle on an everyday basis is limited at best, and a White person who decides that he or she needs to carry a gun to protect themselves is usually thinking about crime and criminals in a racial sense. To deny what I just said is to deny reality, but because this issue was not covered in the NSDS survey, the authors of that survey, Gary Kleck and David Mustard, used their results to paint a picture of gun use which had no basis in fact.

But let's not forget that the sacred texts that enshrine myths don't need to be rooted in fact. All they need is to respond to some emotional need or another which sustains the myth. Which is why this survey, although debunked, derided and dismissed by scores of scholars, some of whom would never consider themselves to be anti-gun, has remained a serious addition to the collection of texts which sustain the armed citizen myth. Kleck himself has admitted that he can't prove beyond a shadow of a doubt that what he said in his survey is actually true. What he falls back on is the idea that nothing proposed by his critics has been shown to be any closer to the truth; at least not to him.[3] What is most interesting in this entire situation, however, is the fact that Kleck, nomenclature to the contrary, has never attempted to repeat his survey methodology again. Nor have any of his political or organizational supporters offered to get on the phones, call up a few hundred randomly-chosen people and see if what they say affirms or negates claims made by Kleck more than twenty years ago.

Actually, that last statement is not entirely true. In 1997, the creator of the second, great mythic text, John Lott, claimed to have conducted his own, private survey which showed that only 15% of individuals who committed DGUs actually shot off their guns. This finding corresponded exactly with what Kleck claimed was the case when he surveyed his DGUs. The only problem was that when Lott was challenged to produce the data behind his finding, he announced that the entire file covering every aspect of the survey had been lost in a hard-drive crash, a statement that elicited criticism both from the Left and the Right, including a negative outburst from Gary Kleck.[4] Over the years Lott has made endless attempts to solicit testimonials from fellow researchers and others to support his claim that the survey data on his hard drive was actually lost. What he been able to verify is the fact that some kind of accident may have occurred that did something to his hard drive; whether there was any survey data on the hard drive has never been declared to be a fact.

But Lott himself was onto bigger game because by the time he allegedly lost the DGU survey insofar as he was busily constructing the second, and in many respects an even more important sacred, armed-citizen text, in this case a book, More Guns, Less Crime.[5] Lott's book, first published in 1998 when the

NRA strategy to push concealed-carry at the state level was in full throttle, advanced the thesis that whenever and wherever states or localities began issuing concealed-carry permits, violent crime rates went down or crime shifted away from face-to-face encounters to crimes against property. In effect, Lott took Kleck's alleged findings about DGUs and extended them to show that legalizing armed citizens was a deterrent to violent crime.

I also deal in detail with Lott's work in The Great American Gun Argument so I'll only give the headlines here. In the same way that I find some of Kleck's basic research model to be so flawed as to render suspect any judgement of the value of his work, I find this to be true of Lott's work as well. In particular, I take exception to the whole notion of criminal behavior displacement which he advances to explain and justify the entire book. By "displacement" what I mean is the idea that criminals would consciously choose to change the modus oprandi of the types of crimes they commit in response to changes in gun licensing laws, which Lott says are most evident in the shift from homicide to property crimes.

The idea that homicide, of all crimes the most impulsive, unplanned and unexplained criminal behavior could be shown to be influenced to any degree by the possibility that, all of a sudden the potential victim might be able to defend himself with a gun is so ludicrous as to make any attempt to use such an assumption as the methodological basis for analyzing cause-and-effect of various trends completely and totally ludicrous. And Lott, even more than Kleck, has come in for a mountain of scholarly criticism, much of it based on the fact that scholars with access to his data have been unable to replicate his results.

But let's say for a moment that Lott is actually correct; that when a community arms itself for purposes of self-defense that criminals look elsewhere to commit crimes because the deterrence represented by a gun is simply too great a risk to justify committing a criminal act. And let's even accept Lott's argument that the reduction in crime that has been caused by the expansion of concealed-carry licensing has been worth six or seven billion annually in cost-savings because a certain number of crimes were not committed; hence property was not damaged, more cops didn't need to be hired, etc.

Such a cost-benefit justification for armed citizens, even if the numbers are true, begs the most important question of all, namely, comparing these cost savings to the expenditures aggregated by the risks embodied in walking around with guns. It would be easy for me, for example, to look at the data presented by the Violence Policy Institute and translate the 70 deaths attributed to CCW-holders in Florida since 2007, (probably underestimated by at least half), figure out the total costs of this carnage and I suspect that it would easily equal or surpass the alleged savings from the growth of concealed-carry licensing in the Sunshine State over the same period of time.

But the fact that most CCW-holders are law-abiding citizens who, as a rule, don't use their guns to commit crimes, even homicide, is not the real issue involved in trying to weigh the costs versus benefits of armed citizens. The real issue, and one which armed citizen proponents like John Lott refuse to discuss, is the risks and costs of more people owning guns because, by definition, if more guns are in circulation, more guns get stolen, more guns get used in crimes, more guns end up causing gun violence costs to go up. In fact, a serious study commissioned by Mother Jones found that the annual cost of gun violence, including the penal costs of jailing the criminals who use guns amounts to more than $229 billion per year, which is so far beyond the alleged savings claimed by Lott as to render his whole cost-benefit analysis of CCW to the realm of the absurd.[6]

One more point needs to be added here not just about Lott, but about the whole issue of armed, self-defense. Most of the eleven, or twelve, or fourteen million people who currently have been issued a concealed-carry license happen to live, work and travel in parts of the country where crimes that might require armed response occur so infrequently that virtually none of the concealed-carry holders will probably ever have any reason to use or carry a gun. With the exception of Arizona, the five states that have taken CCW to its extreme and allow for concealed-carry without any licensing at all (this is known as "constitutional carry," the nirvana of all CCW) have violent crime rates below the national average, and permitless CCW states like Kansas and Wyoming register little, if any gun violence at all. The fact is that there is absolutely no solid evidence connecting the existence of armed citizens to decreases in violent crime for the simple reason that most legal gun owners don't live in high-crime neighborhoods whether they choose to carry a gun or not. But this reality in no way impinged on the mythical fantasy that the NRA and the pro-gun community had been promoting for at least thirty years before the Supreme Court decided to revisit the 2nd Amendment and create the most important mythic legend of all, namely, that Americans had a long tradition of using handguns in self-defense.

When the 2008 Heller decision was announced, the NRA breathed a great sigh of relief. This was because, leading up to the decision, the NRA thought there was a good chance that the Court would re-affirm the previous 2nd-Amendment ruling issued in 1939 (United States v. Miller) in which the Court held that the 2nd Amendment applied only to the bearing of arms for the "collective" defense. The brief submitted by the Solicitor General Robert Jackson (later the head prosecutor at Nuremburg) summed it up best: "Indeed, the very declaration in the Second Amendment that 'a well-regulated Militia, being necessary to the security of a free State,' indicates that the right… is not one which may be utilized for private purposes but only one which exists where the arms are borne in the militia or some other military organization provided for by law and intended for the protection of the state."[7]

The fact that the 2nd Amendment was only considered to extend constitutional protection to guns connected in some way to military service did not, of course, mean that civilian gun ownership in the decades after the Miller decision was either outlawed or in any way threatened by federal or state laws. In fact, the drive to expand legal recognition not only of gun ownership but the right to carry a gun for self-defense both inside and outside the home began to pick up steam several decades prior to the rendering of the Heller decision in 2008.

But the momentum that led to Heller was not so much a steady stream of legal cases that required a new interpretation of the 2nd Amendment, nor was it the degree to which the passage of CCW laws in state after state brought about conflicts in figuring out whether or not the 2nd Amendment could be used to justify more civilian ownership or use of guns. Rather, it was the result of a general growth of conservatism and libertarianism within the ranks of the legal profession itself, which then fastened on the 2nd Amendment as one of the ways in which a more conservative Constitutional stance for all legal matters could be advanced.

Much of this legal activity emerged in the gradual rightward drift of the Federal judiciary with the disappearance of the generation of liberal jurists appointed by Roosevelt and Truman. It became more evident during the Reagan administration with a very pronounced policy of appointing a more conservative judiciary who would follow the dictums of Reagan's Attorney General, Edwin Meese, to interpret the Constitution in as narrow (i.e., conservative) a way as possible. Meese, you may recall, argued again and again that the Bill of Rights did not apply to the States, a position consistent with his "originalist" view of the Constitution which meant that decisions would be bound by the language of the document and the intention of the individuals who wrote it.[8]

Which was exactly the argument made about the 2nd Amendment by Jackson in 1939, namely, that the Framers explicitly tied gun ownership to participation in a militia, because their intention was to maintain state militias as a protection against the possible threat to liberty posed by a national, standing army. And when this originalist approach to the 2nd Amendment was first questioned, it wasn't a question raised by a conservative jurist or scholar, but rather by an extremely liberal legal scholar, Sanford Levinson, in an article published by the Yale Law Journal in 1989.[9]

Before I get into Levinson's text, be advised that there has been an excessive amount of writing on Heller, most of it quite well done on both sides of the issue, and I do not intend to use much space in this book to go over that ground again. The reader will find an extensive bibliography in the notes that accompany Winkler's book, if you care to review even a small portion of what is listed, you will be busily reading for months on end. But I do need to spend a bit of time on Levinson because his approach to the whole issue explains to some degree why I am writing this book myself.

Levinson's article was important for two reasons: First, it appeared at a time when, in the aftermath of the Reagan landslide, New Right legal scholars and public-interest attorneys were trying to shift the entire discussion of all Constitutional issues in a rightward direction, which made the 2nd Amendment grist for their mills. Second, Levinson's article also appeared when, following the 1987 change in Florida's CCW law, the NRA and other pro-gun advocacy groups were mounting a national campaign to enact concealed-carry statutes in all fifty states, using the idea that the 2nd Amendment's protection of individual gun ownership justified laws that allowed citizens to arm themselves with guns.

What Levinson basically argued was that liberal legal scholars like himself, traditionally gave the 2nd Amendment short shrift primarily for socio-cultural reasons, namely, the fact that academics had little or no interest in owning or using guns. This basic shunning of gun culture by liberal faculty and researchers was also not unusual for members of the judiciary, even those known to hold conservative views. Levinson quotes Associate Justice Lewis Powell who, in a speech to the American Bar Association, noted the numbers of murders committed with handguns, saying that "with respect to handguns," in contrast "to sporting rifles and shotguns, it is not easy to understand why the Second Amendment, or the notation of liberty, should be viewed as creating a right to own and carry a weapon that contributes so directly to the shocking number of murders in our society."[10] This is the same Lewis Powell, incidentally, who once sent a confidential memo to a friend at the U.S. Chamber of Commerce advocating the development of a research and advocacy organizational network to counterbalance the anti-capitalist rhetoric and culture that dominated college campuses and mass media in general.[11]

But by conditioning their interpretation of the 2nd Amendment so as to foreclose any Constitutional protection of private gun ownership, conservatives like Powell were using what Levinson called the "significant social cost" argument that liberals usually advanced when defending Constitutional protections that often went against the conservative grain. So, for example, liberal support for the rights of criminal defendants meant accepting the fact that maintaining Constitutional rights might have serious social consequences (such as criminals being set free) which nevertheless had to be endured in order that the Constitution remain the foundational document for all laws of the land.

This basic doctrine, the idea that a Constitutional right must be understood on its own terms regardless of the social consequences of its existence, was clearly behind Scalia's approach to the Heller case. Here is how he states this issue in the final paragraph of his opinion: ". . . the enshrinement of constitutional rights necessarily takes certain policy choices off the table. These include the absolute prohibition of handguns held and used for self-defense in the home."12 But the problem with Scalia's approach is that nowhere in the 2nd Amendment can we find any mention of handguns, no mention anywhere in the Constitution at all. And what made the Heller decision so important from the gun industry's point of view, and the reason the NRA actually was afraid of the case going to the High Court, was because the issue before the Court was not the private ownership of guns per se, but the D.C. law which made it a crime to keep a handgun in the home. Which meant that not only did the Court have to find that the 2nd Amendment validated private ownership of guns entirely disconnected from the actuality or possibility of military service, but it also had to find a Constitutional rationale for what kind of guns could be owned privately and how they could be used.

Notice that in the judicial decisions and commentaries that would be proffered by both sides in the Heller case, virtually all of the verbiage comes down to defining the words "keep" and "bear," as in citizens having the right to keep and bear arms. But there is little, hardly any attempt to define the word "arms." And this is one of the reasons why Scalia was able to construct a myth that could be used to justify the armed citizen because he was able to quickly gloss over any concern about how to define the word "arms" in order to promote and defend his own myth-making version of what the 2nd Amendment really meant. But let's get back for a moment to Levinson.

Because it was Levinson who, knowingly or not, bestowed the liberal imprimatur on what would later become the myth invented by Scalia to define his entire approach to 2nd-Amendment rights. While Levinson's article discussed in detail the traditional disagreement over the meaning of the 2nd Amendment, namely, whether it conferred an individual rather than a collective right to own guns, he ultimately based his entire argument about the Amendment's meaning on the idea that citizens needed some way to protect themselves against what he called the "armed state." And if this mode of protection involved keeping a handgun at the ready to ward off the potential excesses of the national state, the fact that handguns could also be used to kill and maim thousands every year was a price that supporting Constitutional rights required us to pay.

Levinson ends up agreeing with the idea supported by most 2nd-Amendment scholarship that the Framers were reflecting a long line of traditional thinking which posited that guns were necessary to protect individuals from threats against their political well-being, as opposed to threats to their persons or property per se. Citing events in Tianamen Square, Northern Ireland and the Occupied Palestinian Territories, Levinson says, "The fact that these may not be pleasant examples does not affect the principal point, that a state facing a totally disarmed population is in a far better position, for good or ill, to suppress popular demonstrations and uprisings than one that must calculate the possibilities of its soldiers and officials being injured or killed." And if the social cost of giving citizens the potential ability to protect themselves from the state meant accepting everyday carnage committed by personally-owned guns, so be it. The whole point of Constitutional protections, according to Levinson, must always rest on the ideal of freedom itself which cannot be abridged simply because we have to pay a high or burdensome social cost.

Except that was not the basis upon which Scalia analyzed the ultimate defense of the 2nd Amendment as justifying the private ownership of guns so as to let citizens protect themselves against political threats from the state. In fact, Scalia patently ignored an overwhelming scholarly and judicial consensus on what kind of threats could be obviated by personal ownership of guns, preferring instead to focus on the idea that the phrase "keep and bear" meant to use guns for personal, as opposed to political defense. To quote Scalia (at length) on this very point:

> It is no answer to say, as petitioners do, that it is permissible to ban the possession of handguns so long as the possession of other firearms (i.e., long guns) is allowed. It is enough to note, as we have observed, that the American people have considered the handgun to be the quintessential self-defense weapon. There are many reasons that a citizen may prefer a handgun for home defense: It is easier to store in a location that is readily accessible in an emergency; it cannot easily be redirected or wrestled away by an attacker; it is easier to use for those without the upperbody strength to lift and aim a long gun; it can be pointed at a burglar with one hand while the other hand dials the police. Whatever the reason, handguns are the most popular weapon chosen by Americans for

self-defense in the home, and a complete prohibition of their use is invalid.

The DC law that was found unconstitutional in the Heller case banned handgun ownership within the District. It also banned keeping long guns accessible; i.e., unlocked, within the home, even though it did not prevent a DC resident from unlocking, loading and then using a rifle or respond to a real or imagined crime. But what makes Scalia's 2008 opinion the penultimate basis for the armed citizen myth was not the finding that a handgun ban was unconstitutional per se, but his assertion that "handguns are the most popular weapon chosen by Americans for self-defense in the home," a judgment repeated multiple times throughout the opinion text without reference to any informational or expert opinion at all.

Here is the point at which, it seems to me, Scalia knowingly confuses two very different rights; namely, the right to self-defense versus the right to self-defense using a gun. It is the self-same confusion repeated again and again by diehard 2nd Amendment proponents who have tried, often successfully, to push the meaning of the Heller decision far beyond its original bounds. The confusion first appears in the introductory part of Scalia's text: "Respondent [Heller] argues that it [the 2nd Amendment] protects an individual right to possess a firearm unconnected with service in a militia, and to use that arm for traditionally lawful purposes, such as self-defense within the home." But self-defense as a tradition is one thing, self-defense involving the use of a gun is something else. The former can be found in virtually every legal text since the Code of Hammurabi, the latter appears rarely, and when it does appear, the reference invariably is to the use of "arms," with nothing even remotely connected to the ownership or use of handguns as a specific type of arm.

And this is a very important distinction, much more important than what Scalia would have us believe. Because in the Colonial debates about the existence of citizen-militias, as opposed to a national army, which was the context in which the whole notion of the "right to bear arms" was discussed and ultimately codified into Constitutional law, the prevailing opinion was that many of the "arms" owned by civilians weren't, in fact, types of weapons that could be used for military or tactical purposes at all. The guns that were sitting in many colonial homes were poorly-made, often of small caliber for hunting of birds or small game, and they weren't considered proper for use in defending against or attacking other human beings at all.

When the Framers inserted the phrase "keep and bear" within the text of the 2nd Amendment, they weren't thinking about handguns. It's not even clear that they were assuming that when people were called out to serve in the militia, that they would necessarily bring their own weapon along and use it to engage in a fight. But the one thing we do know is that whatever the phrase "keep and bear" meant within the context of ownership of arms, it certainly didn't have anything to do with handguns, either in terms of using them as weapons of war or for personal defense.

Scalia goes into great detail to show that, from well before Colonial times, the keeping and bearing of arms was considered a personal right. He then surveys both legal literature and judicial history from the early times through the 1939 Miller decision and finds again and again that the notion of gun ownership assumed an individual, not a collective right. But at no point in this entire discourse on what "keep and bear" really means does Scalia produce a single tract which indicates that handguns were necessarily protected because citizens were allowed to keep and bear "arms." So how does he manage to fit the notion of using handguns for personal defense into his overall scheme?

He comes up with the idea that the 2nd Amendment specifically protects handgun use for self-defense by asserting, as I said earlier, that handguns have become the "quintessential," or "traditional," type of weapon used for self-defense. Therefore, since the law recognizes self-defense as a longstanding right, and since the 2nd Amendment gives everyone the right to keep a gun in their home for personal defense, and since the most frequent type of gun that is kept in the home happens to be a handgun, ipso facto, the 2nd Amendment allows people to use a handgun for self-defense. Voila! The myth of the armed citizen has emerged and Americans have the Constitutional right to defend themselves (and others) not just with a gun, but with a handgun.

Why is it a myth? For two reasons. First, the myth follows from Scalia's statement at the outset of his brief that the case would be decided not on whether someone could keep a gun in their home for self-defense, but whether someone could keep a "usable" handgun in their home for self-defense. DC law allowed residents to keep long guns in their homes, as long as the guns were rendered unusable through the installation of a trigger lock or some other device. But Heller's defense team chose not to decide the case based on whether a DC resident could keep a long gun in the home to defend against crime; they were specifically seeking constitutional legal protection for what Scalia referred to as a "whole class of weapons" that could be used in self-defense, namely handguns. And while Heller could have sued the District to let him keep an unlocked rifle or shotgun at the ready, a suit he later entered and lost, he and his legal team chose to argue for 2nd-Amendment protection of his revolver, because the law Scalia would throw out already gave Heller the right to keep rifles and shotguns in his home.

The second, and more important reason behind Scalia's creation of the myth, however, lay in how he responded to the minority who were overruled in this decision and, in particular, the approach to the case by Associate Justice Breyer, whose reasoning and argument gave Scalia the real basis on which he could build his myth. What I am saying is that for all the talk about how the Heller decision was a triumph of the general rightward drift of the Court and the ascendance, at least in this instance of the originalist Constitutionalist ideal, in fact, the pro-gun community owes the existence of the armed-citizen myth much more to how a liberal named Stephen Breyer framed his views on gun ownership than anything Scalia ever said.

Breyer's dissent focused basically on the motives behind DC's decision to outlaw the ownership of handguns, a decision based primarily on the level of criminal violence associated with handguns over the previous years. He noted that while the District City Council couldn't definitively prove that making the city a gun-free zone would result in less gun violence, there was nothing to prevent the city government from taking this step if they believed they were responding to a problem in a manner that was consistent with normal governmental reactions to any issue that fell under the government's control.

For Breyer, the fact that DC residents could still use a rifle or a shotgun to defend themselves in their homes against personal threats was, in and of itself, enough justification for believing that banning a different class of weapons – handguns – did not remove 2nd Amendment protections for gun ownership from residents of DC. But his rationale for stripping handguns from law-abiding citizens ultimately came down to exactly the issue which Sanford Levinson warned liberals to avoid arguing in debates about the 2nd Amendment, namely, the idea that supporting or denying a Constitutional right could not be based on whether the outcome protected by that right was good or bad.

Here is Breyer's attempt to explain the rationale for banning handguns in DC, and therefore his judgment that such a ban would not undermine the Constitutional right to own a gun:

But I cannot understand how one can take from the elected branches of government the right to decide whether to insist upon a handgun-free urban populace in a city now facing a serious crime problem and which, in the future, could well face environmental or other emergencies that threaten the breakdown of law and order.

And here is Scalia's response:

But the enshrinement of constitutional rights necessarily takes certain policy choices off the table. These include the absolute prohibition of handguns held and used for self-defense in the home. Undoubtedly some think that the Second Amendment is outmoded in a society where our standing army is the pride of our Nation, where well-trained police forces provide personal security, and where gun violence is a serious problem. That is perhaps debatable, but what is not debatable is that it is not the role of this Court to pronounce the Second Amendment extinct.

So what we end up with in Heller is a conservative justice using a liberal argument for declaring a Constitutional right to own a gun. And what was Scalia's ultimate rationale for springing the trap which a reading of Levinson's analysis of the 2nd Amendment allowed him to set? The idea that handguns were not only a favored method for protecting hearth and home, but a "traditional" method as well. And where did this tradition come from? From Scalia's decision to create the armed citizen myth and nothing else. Unless, of course, you want to argue that we should call a certain type of behavior "traditional" when it has been in general use for perhaps no more than twenty years and was certainly not employed by a majority of citizens, perhaps not even a majority of citizens who owned guns.

Scalia's creation of an armed citizen myth based on the idea of citizens using handguns to protect themselves is not only false in terms of how and when the "tradition" of armed, personal defense really came to exist, but it's also false based on the rationale he presented for accepting handguns as being a normal or usual type of weapon at all. The problem here involves a recognition on his part that the 2nd Amendment had to be defined in a way that would allow for private ownership but would still let the government, to a certain extent, regulate guns. After all, had Scalia walked into the conference where this case was discussed and announced that the government had no right to involve itself in anything having to do with guns, he would have quickly lost at least two votes of his pro-gun group (Roberts and Kennedy) and perhaps one more. So he had to find some way to balance out the competing interests of the government to regulate guns and the interests of gun nuts like himself to enshrine and protect private gun ownership, and the way he did that was to go back to the 1939 *Miller* case which rested on a definition of guns "in common use" at that time.

Miller involved the Arkansas prosecution of two individuals – Jack Miller and Frank Layton – for carrying a sawed-off shotgun across a state line. The defendants argued that the National Firearms Act of 1934 violated their 2nd-Amendment rights because they were denied the legal ownership of this particular type of gun. The 1934 NFA was passed basically to regulate weapons that had been used by gangsters during Prohibition, in particular machine guns and sawed-off shotguns, both of which were carried by the Capone Mob and other criminals popularized by the Untouchables, Eliot Ness and the whole popular culture of gangsters that began to draw Hollywood's attention in the decade after Prohibition came to an end.

It was in this context that the Court decided that Miller and Layton were not protected by the 2nd

Amendment since the weapon they were carrying was outlawed by the 1934 NFA because it wasn't considered to be a "normal" or "usual" type of gun. And this is where Scalia drew the distinction between the *Miller* and *Heller* cases, namely, that the 2nd Amendment protected guns that were considered "usual" or "typical" guns owned by Americans, which could not be said about sawed-off shotguns, but would certainly apply to handguns and rifles, particularly those guns which Americans "traditionally" used for self-defense.

And the degree to which handguns were allegedly used for self-defense was supplied by Heller's attorney, Alan Gura, who told the Court that handguns represented 40% of all guns owned by civilians, and were used for self-defense in 80% of all cases of self-defense. Which is probably true, except that Gura's testimony and Scalia's promotion of handguns as the "quintessential' method for armed self-defense begs a much bigger question, namely, whether guns and self-defense have anything to do with each other at all. The fact that most self-defense gun use involved handguns is, after all, of little consequence if the number of such events is small. And the verified number of times that guns of any type are used in self-defense makes a mockery of the whole attempt to connect guns to personal protection against crime.

What ultimately makes Scalia the creator of the biggest gun myth of all is not the fact that he defined the 2nd Amendment as a personal right when historical texts did not support such a claim at all; nor the fact that he pronounced that ownership of personal-defense handguns to be a long-standing American tradition which it wasn't; nor even his idea that a handgun was better suited than a rifle for personal-defense because of its size and versatility – just try to get *that* one past the AR-15 folks. Nope. Those were only secondary reasons proffered by Scalia to support his grand myth.

What Scalia was protecting with his myth was not a certain class of people who kept handguns in their homes for self-defense; he was really protecting a certain class of people who believed that they needed some kind, any kind of protection because otherwise they would become the victims of a personal attack. Because the fact is that the decision by any American to become an armed citizen ultimately rested on the notion, promoted vigorously and continuously by the NRA, that sooner or later they would all be victimized by a personal assault (Cooper's declaration about the ubiquity of "human savagery" is relevant here) for which the best and most obvious form of defense was access to a handgun protected by a Constitutional right.

And in case you still don't understand what happens to people who don't have access to guns to protect themselves against the "savagery" of human existence, I'm going to tell you in the next chapter about two human communities whose entire existence was allegedly threatened and almost destroyed because they didn't enjoy the Constitutional protection of armed-defense.

CHAPTER 5

EXAMPLES OF THE MYTH

Now that we have a sacred text for the "armed citizen" myth, what will strengthen the myth is to show what happened when people didn't believe it and didn't follow it. And this recounting has been built around two historical events which are perfect motifs for explaining not only the value of following the myth, but the horrendous results that befall people who don't follow the myth. The first and most horrendous example involves the Holocaust, a.k.a. the destruction of the European Jews. Between the advent of the Nazi regime in 1933 until the war came to an end in 1945, the Nazis killed more than 5 million Jews, most of them perishing in concentration camps after 1942.[1] In order to massacre this population, the Nazis had to round them up in the cities and villages in which they lived, then transport them to a concentration camp, which was usually hundreds of miles from their place of settlement, then herd the Jews into the camps and then methodically murder them on a continuous, mass scale.

Most of this enormous movement of populations through lands occupied by the Reich was effected by military units, either local units under Nazi authority or by the German military itself. And in every single instance, an individual, a family, an entire community had to be physically uprooted from where they lived, marched to a transportation center, herded onto trains and transported to a camp. And although it took some time until it was clear that moving this vast population was not being done for purposes of "resettlement," there is no indication that Jews from the beginning viewed this process in a particularly benign way.

At the same time, there is little, if any indication that Jewish communities attempted a significant degree of resistance to this forced relocation with the exception of the uprising which took place in the Polish town of Warsaw in 1943.[2] The resistance against the Nazi plan to transport the Jewish population of Warsaw to the Treblinka concentration camp broke out on April 19 and lasted until May 16. The German military forces that attacked the ghetto fighters numbered some 2,000 troops armed with rifles, flame-throwers, grenade-launchers and light machine guns; the type of weaponry that would be used against urban guerrilla forces who had to be fought on a house-to-house basis. When the fighting ended, the commander of the German forces, Jurgen Stroop, estimated that his men had faced somewhere around 200 resistance fighters armed with as few as 10 rifles, 60 handguns and a variety of homemade bombs and explosives, along with a few grenades and other light ordnance captured from the Germans during the fight.

The fact that the liquidation of the Warsaw Ghetto took less than two months is a testament to the degree to which the German military authorities did not consider the armed Jewish response to deportations from Warsaw to be a serious military affair. I'm not denigrating the heroism of the Jewish fighters in any way shape or form; I am simply commenting on the degree to which the uprising could not have been successful through force of arms. And while there were other instances of Jewish communities attempting physical resistance to deportations in Vilna, Tarnow, Kremenets, Bialystok and Mir, at no point did any of these uprisings pose the slightest military threat to the Final Solution carried out by the Nazis following the Wannsee Conference in 1942.

The idea that gun control is a sure-fire path towards totalitarianism and tyranny has been embedded in the lexicon of the pro-gun movement since there ever was a pro-gun movement. Much of this rhetoric floats around on various paranoid right-wing internet blogs and sites devoted to every type of nut-job, conspiracy theories which exist. But to the extent that 2nd-Amendment supporters view themselves as helping to secure our basic freedoms through gun ownership, obviously the government that would trample on those freedoms would, by definition, take the guns away. It's a simplistic view of history and current political events, but the NRA has been selling this line since it got into the gun-control debate big-time after the passage of GCA68.

But since neither universal (or even partial) civilian disarmament nor the abolition of elections has yet occurred in the United States, if you want to give an example of what happens in places where the government has created unarmed citizens, thus helping to validate the armed citizen myth, you have to look somewhere else. And what better place is there to look than the experiences of Jews under Nazi rule? And the alleged history of how Jews were slaughtered by the Nazis after they were made defenseless by being disarmed is the subject of a book written by an attorney who just happens to work as a legal counsel for the NRA.

If there's a media program about the 2nd Amendment, there's a good chance you'll see and hear Stephen Halbrook, who has cobbled together a very impressive resume which includes arguments for gun rights before various Federal and State courts, appearances on all the requisite Fox talk shows, *amicus briefs* filed here and there in a variety of gun-rights cases and a book entitled *Gun Control in the Third Reich*.[3] Incidentally, before I get into Halbrook's attempt to promote the "armed citizen" myth through a strong but historically misplaced argument about disarming the Jews, I do need to give this attorney his just due and mention his work as the legal representative for Jaime Castillo, whose weapons conviction after Waco was yet another terrible part of a government-led event that was wrong from end to end.[4] And since I have written at length about the ATF bungling in Volume 5, I am particularly sensitive to how this mess eventually played out.

Castillo was a survivor of the Waco massacre but was arrested, charged with using a machine gun during the siege of the compound and sentenced to thirty years. The whole machine gun issue was entirely bogus to begin with and I do not know whether the government actually proved that Castillo had used a full-auto gun. But no matter, he was sent off for a long stretch without benefit of a jury trial which, according to the motion filed by Halbrook, was not the way in which the law under which he was tried could even be used. In effect, the government took the "type" of firearm (in this case a so-called machine gun) and made it into a specific offense, whereas the law only used that term to denote the character of the weapon rather than making the use of a specific type of gun a separate crime in and of itself. Castillo had already served two years beyond the five-year sentence that he should have served for using any kind of gun to commit a violent crime, thus, the Court's decision immediately ended what would have been an incarceration that otherwise could have dragged on for another twenty-three years.

So score one for Halbrook on the matter of Castillo and Waco. When it comes to his argument about disarming the Jews and the Holocaust however, his views may help promote the idea that the Nazi genocide was made an easier task because the victims of that genocide didn't have the means to defend themselves, but like so much of the argument made by the pro-gun community about the values and virtues of armed, self-defense, it's simply not true.

According to Halbrook, the entire issue went back to a gun-control law passed in the pre-Nazi period by the Weimar government that was aimed primarily at disarming political opponents to the regime. The Weimar Republic, you may recall, came into power after World War I and immediately faced serious political opposition both from the Left and the Right. Within a year after coming to power, the government found itself unable to control what became increasingly violent-prone political demonstrations and events, including widespread labor strikes and unrest, along with pitched street battles between political adversaries that often resulted in serious levels of injury and general unrest.

In response to growing political disturbances and a real fear that the government would not be able to maintain control over the general populace, the government passed a firearms law in 1928 which by 1931 was expanded to allow the police to confiscate privately-owned guns as well as to maintain lists of civilians who owned guns. The 1931 law also banned political demonstrations without prior governmental permission, although this provision of the law was basically ignored, in particular by the Nazi party which was gradually consolidating political strength partly through continuous street violence against various Leftist unions and political groups.

The civilian disarmament which accompanied the rise of the Nazi regime in fact occurred with the passage of the Weapons Law in 1938. The law, as developed by Nazi Interior Minister Wilhelm Frick, was aimed at "enemies of the people and the state and other elements that pose a danger to public security." It did not mention street crime or common criminality at all. The law also established a licensing requirement for gun ownership and defined certain groups who could not obtain a license, again for the most part defining such groups as constituting a political threat to the ruling hegemony of the Nazi regime.

The 1938 law was adopted in March, and it was followed in November of the same year by a governmental decree that banned Jewish ownership of all weapons. In the intervening eight months, the regime had stepped up both the legal and social elements of anti-Semitism, most notoriously a series of anti-Jewish riots and attacks against Jewish property that led up to the widespread destruction and wholesale arrests of Jews during the infamous *Kristallnacht* on November 9-10. The decree banning Jewish ownership of all guns followed directly after this event.

In reviewing this entire episode of gun laws and confiscations from Weimar through the Nazi period, NRA consul Halbrook sums it up as follows: "firearms prohibitions nipped in the bud the possibility of a popular armed resistance movement and insured in particular that no armed Jewish resistance to the Holocaust could arise. Armed opposition was limited to isolated instances of individuals resisting deportation, together with loners and Wehrmacht officers unsuccessfully trying to kill Hitler."

In 2008, five years before Halbrook decided that the Holocaust was successful because the Jews didn't have guns, the following email floated all over the internet, including my Outlook Inbox:

A LITTLE GUN HISTORY

I Thought you might appreciate this . .In 1929, the Soviet Union established gun control. From 1929 to 1953, about 20 million dissidents, unable to defend themselves, were rounded up and exterminated.

In 1911, Turkey established gun control. From 1915 to 1917, 1.5 million
Armenians, unable to defend themselves, were rounded
up and exterminated.

Germany established gun control in 1938 and from 1939 to 1945, a total of
13 million Jews and others who were unable to defend themselves were
rounded up and exterminated.

China established gun control in 1935. From 1948 to 1952, 20 million
political dissidents, unable to defend themselves, were rounded up and

exterminated.

Guatemala established gun control in 1964. From 1964 to 1981, 100,000
Mayan Indians, unable to defend themselves, were rounded up and exterminated.

Uganda established gun control in 1970. From 1971 to 1979, 300,000
Christians, unable to defend themselves, were rounded up and exterminated.

Cambodia established gun control in 1956. From 1975 to 1977, one million
"educated" people, unable to defend themselves, were rounded up and
exterminated.

------------------ -----------

Defenseless people rounded up
and exterminated in the 20th Century because of gun control = 56 million.

Apparently using this email as his script, Joe "Da Plumber" Wurzelbacher, released a political video that same year in an unsuccessful campaign for Congress in which he not only re-stated most of the erroneous facts in the above email, but promised American Jews that he would defend them in the event of a neo-Nazi takeover of the federal government. A slightly more sophisticated version of this nonsense is regularly pandered on Fox by one of the pro-gun commentators, Andrew Napolitano, who argues that the Warsaw Ghetto uprising is the "proof" that Jews could have successfully resisted their genocide if they had not been forced to give up their arms.

So the guy who wrote the original internet email is a bone-fide member of the idiot lunatic fringe and Napolitano panders to that segment all the time. But now we have an attorney, counsel to the NRA, who has written some serious legal briefs about gun law and, as I indicated above, won an important case on civil liberties before the Supreme Court, and he's promoting the same nonsense over again. It is simply preposterous to assume that in a country like Germany, which never had a tradition of gun ownership beyond hunting rifles and shotguns, that an "armed" citizenry, particularly an urbanized, educated professional population like the German Jews (who didn't, for the most part hunt anyway) could have mounted any serious defense against the Final Solution. Let's not forget, incidentally, that most of the 5 million Jews liquidated in the killing camps lived outside of Germany (mostly in Poland) where they, like the rest of the populations in occupied Europe, found themselves facing a level of military power that had easily dismembered their own, local armed forces. And Jews or anyone else armed with handguns were going to represent an "armed resistance" force against Panzers?

But let's pause for a moment and give Halbrook and the disarmament = totalitarianism gang the benefit of the doubt and assume that governments that want to strip citizens of their basic civil rights can be counted on to also take away the guns. After all, a well-meaning, anti-gun liberal like Levinson argues the same thing. There's only one little problem. From the first gun-control law passed by Roosevelt in 1934, through the most recent gun-control effort by Obama after Sandy Hook, the justification for every one of these laws was to curb ordinary crime and the behavior of ordinary criminals. There has never been any gun control law of any kind that came out of concerns that allowing private citizens to own guns represented a political threat to the political authority of the state. Conversely, there was not a single concern among the Nazi officials who developed their gun-control laws that they were worried about the use of guns in ordinary crime.

What further weakens the cause-and-effect argument between disarming the Jews and sending them to killing camps is the fact that the non-Jewish German population, most of whom were allowed to own and keep private guns, never made any attempt to engage in armed resistance against the Nazi regime, even when virtually all civil liberties and freedoms were abolished during the war itself. I'm not saying that Germany's non-Jewish population ever experienced anything remotely similar to what happened to Germany's Jews with the deportations beginning at the end of 1942. But the Nazi regime, particularly during its waning years, did not behave benignly towards anyone – it was a brutal, military dictatorship that suffered no disputes or challenges to its rule.

In the case of the Holocaust, the attempt to use the "armed citizen" myth as a mechanism for understanding the impact on society when the right to self-defense with guns has been taken away by the government has never been an official part of the NRA's storybook to promote gun ownership. But this is not the case when it comes to the NRA's effort to promote gun ownership among African-Americans which constitutes another non-gun population that seems largely resistant to the notion of using guns for self-protection, even if the crime data demonstrates the evident fact that African-Americans are so frequently the victims of violent crime.

The NRA has what could be politely called an "ambivalent" relationship with the African-American community which stems from the organization's decision in the late 1970s and early 1980s to begin promoting gun ownership as a response to crime. And the crime for which guns could provide a measure of security was street crime, a.k.a. violent crimes committed by Blacks. The fact that most violent crime was and still is intra-racial and not inter-racial didn't prevent the NRA from running television spots which were clearly aimed at generating fear of crimes committed by Blacks against Whites, particularly following the Rodney King riots in 1982. Heston's most notorious effort in this regard was a television spot that showed him walking at night through a darkened part of the DC ghetto while intoning that the streets once "ruled by Jefferson, Lincoln and Truman were now ruled by criminals."

Meanwhile, what the NRA was not telling its membership back in the "crime" days was the fact that the notion of armed citizens as representing a force for good was, in fact, developing in the African-American community in response to threats from Whites during the initial conflicts over civil rights. The political militancy of the Black community that began to develop in the 1950's was not just a function of legal victories, such as the 1953 *Brown vs. Board of Education* decision, but reflected the significant participation of Black soldiers in WWII, along with the integration of industrial plants during and after the War. Black veterans returned from service both in the World War and Korea, they were trained in the use of firearms and they often brought the guns back with them. And even though the civil rights movement increasingly followed the civil disobedience teachings and strategies of Martin Luther King, Jr and his associates, one of the earliest disputes about centering on the use of public accommodations involved the very public display and threatened use of guns by Black civil rights organizers.

I am referring here to the decision by Robert Williams, President of the Monroe, NC Chapter of the NAACP, to carry a Colt 45 pistol, and ultimately threaten to use it against a Monroe policeman during a fracas that occurred during demonstrations to desegregate the town swimming pool in 1961. Williams came back to live in Monroe after working in an integrated Detroit factory and then doing a tour in the Marines. He joined and then led the local NAACP branch which began a campaign to integrate the town swimming pool in 1957. Over the next four years Monroe was the scene of numerous racial confrontations caused both by the activism of the NAACP and the resistance of a large Klan contingent which had connections both in the town government and the police.

In addition to facing the anger and threats of local racists, Williams also found himself at odds with African-American organizations, in particular the growing pacifism of the civil rights movement as expressed by Martin Luther King. In 1959, King wrote an article for *Liberation* magazine, and described his differences with Williams' promotion of armed, self-defense in the following way:

> One must be clear that there are three different views on the subject of violence. One is the approach of pure nonviolence, which cannot readily or easily attract large masses, for it requires extraordinary discipline and courage. The second is violence exercised in self-defense, which all societies from the most primitive to the most cultured and civilized, accept as moral and legal. The principle of self-defense, even involving weapons and bloodshed, had never been condemned, even by Gandhi, who sanctioned it for those unable to master pure nonviolence. The third is the advocacy of violence as a tool of advancement, organized as in warfare, deliberately and consciously. To this tendency many Negroes are being tempted today.[5]

The philosophical split between King and Williams never materialized into an organizational quarrel because Williams was forced to leave the country in 1961 to avoid a trumped-up kidnapping charge which was ultimately dropped after he returned to Monroe in 1969. During his residence in Cuba, he published a book, *Negroes With Guns,* which became in many respects the watchword to justify arming the African-American community for self-defense. In fact, when Williams first returned to Monroe in 1955, he requested and received a local chapter charter from – the NRA!

As to whether the direction and strategy of the civil rights movement would be defined by King's appeal to non-violence or Williams' belief in armed, self-defense, here is the latter's reply to King's appeal for the civil rights struggle to flow from non-violent ideals:

> Why do the white liberals ask us to be non-violent? We are not the aggressors; we have been victimized for over 300 years! Yet nobody spends money to go into the South and ask the racists to be martyrs or pacifists. But they always come to the downtrodden Negroes, who are already oppressed and too submissive as a group, and they ask them not to fight back.[6]

While most of the civil rights movement, in particular the leaders who followed MLK tended to downplay or ignore Williams' call to arms, a younger, more militant and armed organization – the Black Panthers – appeared in California in 1966 and quickly spread to more than 60 cities throughout the United States, although their power base remained on the West Coast. Their major leader, Huey Newton, claimed to have been inspired by Williams, adopted many of his slogans and openly carried firearms, including an armed, but peaceful sit-in of the California Assembly in May, 1967, an event sparked by the debate and then passage of the *Mulford Act*, which forbade the open carrying of guns in California, a law that was signed by then-Governor Ronald Reagan and was aimed directly at groups like the Panthers who used the public display of guns to underscore their concerns about being attacked and victimized by the police.

In 1969, when the Panthers were beginning to fall apart due to the arrest of most of their leadership as well as infiltration and counter-intelligence activities by the FBI, the Los Angeles group got into a five-hour shootout with the LAPD in which more than five thousand rounds were fired back and forth between the cops and a group of Panthers holed up in a bungalow at 41st Street in South-Central LA. Nobody was killed in the incident and the Mayor, Sam Yorty, had the good sense to refuse an offer from then-Defense Secretary Mel Laird to send in airborne troops to "calm" things down. And while in the aftermath the Black Panther Party more or less went out of business within the next decade, the image of African-Americans engaged in wholesale, armed defense became fixed in popular culture both within and without the United States.

This image, of course, began to fade alongside the gradual disappearance of the legal and cultural barriers that circumscribed so much of African-American life in the post-War decades. The same town that resisted efforts to integrate the public pool now features a photograph of an African-American putting out on a green at the Monroe Country Club while a White member obligingly holds the flag. When Robert Williams armed NAACP members to resist the Klan, the only Blacks who could be found at the country club were the caddies who toted the bags of the all-white membership from hole to hole.

Now that two generations have come and gone since the racial turbulence of the 50s and 60s, it's quite easy to create a new history of past events which may or may not have anything to do with why and how those events actually occurred. And, like the case of the European Jews who might have been a bulwark against Nazi rule if they had only been armed, so an even more beguiling historical fantasy is being spread by the NRA about the use of guns by African-Americans to protect themselves in the South. In early 2015 the Library of Congress opened a display of writings and pictures devoted to Rosa Parks, the iconic figure who started the Montgomery Bus Boycott in 1955, an event which ushered in the wave of civil rights activity that culminated in the laws signed by Lyndon Johnson in 1964 and 1965. Ironically, Parks delivered the eulogy for Robert Williams who died in 1996.

In the papers collected by the Library of Congress, researchers found references to guns kept in the homes where she was raised, including a statement that her grandfather "kept his shotgun within hand reach at all times." The NRA's discussion about the Rosa Parks archive contains the following:

Stories like Parks', where firearms were used to protect against racially motivated violence before and during the Civil Rights Era, are common. At a time when law enforcement officials were sometimes indifferent to acts of violence perpetrated against African-Americans (or in some cases even complicit in them), those seeking any protection at all had few other options. History could certainly have been altered in dramatic fashion had the Parks home been left undefended against the depredations of the Klan. Thankfully, Parks' family had access to an effective means of self-defense, even as they strove to obtain other basic human rights.

The NRA's tribute to Parks also mentions the organization's awarding of its affiliation to Robert Williams, and concludes by saying, "The story of armed self-defense revealed in the Rosa Parks Collection is a welcome and important addition to the already well-established history of the use of arms to deter and defend against racially-motivated violence."

The discovery of African-American armed, self-defense is the title and theme of a book by Nicholas Johnson, a professor of law at Fordham University, who also happens to be Black and his book, *Negroes and the Gun, The Black Tradition of Arms*, is promoted by the NRA and pro-gun bloggers as an antidote to the gun-control positions usually taken by African-American politicians and community organizations.[7] The book "chronicles a tradition of church folk, merchants, and strivers, the very best people in the community, armed and committed to the principle of individual self-defense." And while Johnson acknowledges that using arms appears contradictory to the "dominant narrative of nonviolence" that characterized the civil rights movement, he claims that while non-violence was a strategy for securing rights, the use of arms was recognized as a valid method for self-defense. He quotes Fannie Lou Hamer in this regard: "'I keep a shotgun in every corner of my bedroom and the first cracker even look like he wants to throw some dynamite on my porch won't write his mama again.'"

Johnson's book is a compilation of well-researched stories about Black resistance to lynchings, riots and other racist attacks from before the Civil War up through the civil rights era. Many of the incidents he uncovers have not previously been studied or have been understated in the accepted historiography covering African-American resistance to racism both in the North and the South. It is an impressive compilation of primary and secondary sources, and probably would have achieved much greater recognition were it not for the fact that mainstream opinion on the issue of Blacks and guns is basically anti-gun.

And the reason that public opinion about minorities and guns tends to be negative is because, by and large, the individuals, groups and organizations that speak out about guns also tend to be anti-gun. There are a few African-American gun clubs here and there, and something called the *National African American Gun Association* has a very impressive website, but walk around any grass-roots gun meeting or even a national gun conclave like SHOT or the NRA, and most of the black faces on the exhibit floor belong to the guys employed by the convention center to move things from here to there. The NRA claims that minorities comprise 15% of their members, but they also claim that one-third of their membership are Democrats. These numbers may help them sell their mail lists to advertisers hawking wine or lawn chairs or whatever else various manufacturers try to sell via the NRA. But it's pretty tough to connect to a minority audience when you've spent the last thirty years telling everyone in America that your organization is first and foremost a bulwark against crime.

The armed citizen myth doesn't apply to the experience of African-Americans with guns for one simple reason, namely, that the decision by African-Americans to use guns for self-defense was, ironically, what the Framers of the Constitution meant when they wrote the 2nd Amendment. In other words, the use by individuals of armed force to protect themselves from political threats; i.e., terrorism as a means of instituting and maintaining some kind of political status quo. In the case of colonial America it was the use of guns to fight against British troops. In the case of African-Americans, it was the use of guns to fight against the Klan.

If pro-gun scholars like Nicholas Johnson or pro-gun video personalities like Colion Noir believe that telling inner-city African-American residents that using guns to protect themselves from crime is simply part and parcel of a long tradition of African-American armed defense, then they don't have the slightest idea about what constitutes historical method or they are consciously perpetuating an intellectual fraud. Either way, their efforts represent another effort to extend and embellish the armed citizen myth with about as much reality behind their arguments as what is found behind most myths that circulate today.

Much the same can be said about the attempt to argue against gun registration by citing the alleged defenselessness of the Jews under the Nazi regime. The decision by the Nazi government to disarm Jews had nothing whatsoever to do with taking guns away from people who might otherwise have constituted a threat to public safety because they were using guns to engage in crime. Jews, like Communists, were seen as political opponents of the Nazi regime and denying them the right to own guns was in keeping with a whole swath of anti-Semitic laws that were designed to prevent them from enjoying the basic privileges that Aryan citizens enjoyed; i.e., business ownership, university enrollment, professional occupations, etc. Meanwhile, the Nazis had no difficulty allowing Aryan citizens to own guns while, at the same time they were demolishing virtually every democratic institution that had characterized the previous Weimar government which they replaced in 1933. I have yet to see a single, pro-NRA or pro-gun advocate admit or even acknowledge that the Nazis had no trouble constructing a totalitarian regime when 99% of the country's population remained in possession of arms – Jews constituting about 1% of Germany's total population in the period prior to World War II.

But the fact that I can use history to refute myth doesn't say anything about the strength of the myth. People are persuaded not by what they know but what they believe. And the gun industry, with the help of acolytes like Antonin Scalia, has shown itself to have an uncanny ability to promote its products to an audience that wants to believe more than anything else that guns represent a measure of security that is more valuable than anything else. They don't hold to this belief because of facts, or history or anything else that can be analyzed in objective terms. They believe it because they want to believe it. Which is what I will discuss in the final chapter of this book.

CHAPTER 6

WHAT SUSTAINS THE MYTH?

Here are the relevant dates and events that brought about the birth, growth and full maturation of the armed citizen myth:

1977 – Election of Harlon Carter as NRA head and beginnings of NRA shift from a hunting/sport organization to an organization that promoted self-defense.

1987 – Passage of Florida concealed-carry law that became a template for CCW laws ultimately passed in more than 30 states.

1995 – Gary Kleck published telephone survey and claims that more than 2 million crimes are prevented each year by DGUs.

1998 – John Lott publishes *More Guns, Less Crime,* which shows correlation between increase in CCW and decrease in violent crime.

2008 – *District of Columbia v. Heller* decision.

2012 – Massacre at Sandy Hook.

Why do I say that the armed citizen myth reached its zenith with the massacre at Sandy Hook? For two reasons. First, in the immediate aftermath of the tragedy, Wayne LaPierre went on a national media blitz and proclaimed that Sandy Hook was the penultimate vindication of an armed citizen strategy because, according to him, Adam Lanza would not have been able to kill the teachers and kids the elementary school had there been an armed presence somewhere in or around the building. And while his battle cry about how only a good guy with a gun can stop a bad guy with a gun had been floating around gun-advocacy circles for at least twenty years, it now became the guiding principle not just for the lobbying strategy of the NRA and other pro-gun advocacy organizations, but as well the defining approach to product development and marketing for the gun industry as a whole.

As an example of the latter, let's briefly explore the product history of America's premier gun maker, *Sturm, Ruger & Co.* The company was founded in 1949 by Bill Ruger and Alex Sturm, the latter a member of an illustrious, Connecticut-Yankee family who put up the seed money for the company; the former a Brooklyn-born engineer who has to be considered as perhaps the foremost American gun designer of all time, second only in influence to John Browning.

Ruger's early guns, including the Mark I, 22-caliber pistol, the 10/22 autoloading, 22-caliber rifle, the Number One single-shot rifle and the single-action Blackhawk revolver were all original designs, filled or created product niches in the small arms industry, and were especially created for the shooting and hunting markets. Ruger himself was an avid hunter and sportsman, had a keen sense for what types of guns would sell to the sporting market, and never felt the need to move the company into military or law enforcement markets, which had been the traditional path to financial success of companies like Smith & Wesson and Colt.

In 1967 the company produced a .223-caliber, semi-automatic rifle known as the Mini-14, which remains one of its best-selling products to this day. The gun was chambered in what had just become the standard U.S. military battle caliber, but the rifle was not at all similar to the AR-style rifles manufactured by Colt and other companies for both civilian and military use; rather, it was a lightweight, semi-automatic hunting gun whose flat-shooting caliber was perfectly suited for smaller game, in particular "nuisance" predators like coyotes that preyed on livestock around a ranch. In fact, the gun was called a "ranch rifle" because it could easily be carried inside a small truck or on a horse. And what this gun represented was the epitome of Bill Ruger's imagination as regards the use of small arms; i.e., take a caliber that has come into favor and adapt it to a hunting or sporting type of gun.

By the time of Ruger's death in 2002, the company was the largest producer of small arms in the United States primarily because its catalog carried virtually every type of gun – revolver, pistol, semi-automatic rifle, bolt-action rifle, shotgun – that shooters could use for any type of hunting or sport. And even as the gun industry began to shift away from a reliance on this market Ruger himself stood firm; up to and including publicly advocating magazine capacity limitations in 1987, a stance that would have caused anyone else in the gun industry severe problems, but in his case basically the issue was ignored. Not even the NRA was about to square off against someone as iconic as Bill Ruger.

The Ruger company is still far and away the largest gun manufacturer in North America, and continues to turn out products in every shooting category. But increasingly the company makes and promotes guns that more in line with the current wave of tactical and self-defense weapons, including AR-style rifles and polymer-frame, concealable pistols, the latter including several guns that are literally a fraction of the size and weight of the more traditional, double-action pistols that Ruger brought to the market in the 1980s when all the American gun makers had to respond to the invasion of hi-cap pistols from overseas. The 9mm SR pistol is considered the quintessential concealable gun, weighing only one pound and measuring less than one inch in width; there is no other weapon of this small size and quality to match it in any market.

Want to prove the old adage that a picture is worth a thousand words? Here's the first page from the 1985 Ruger catalog:

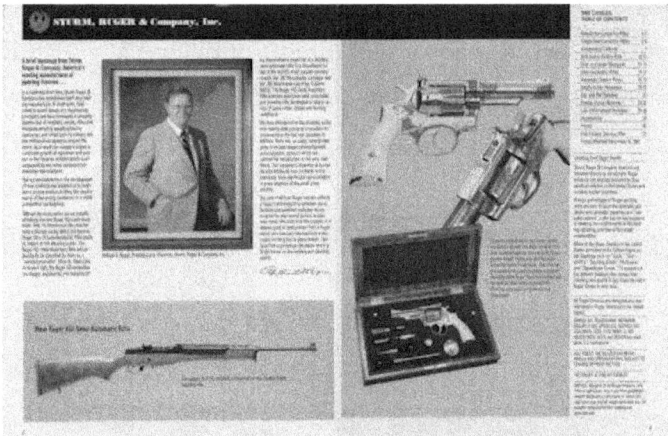

The rifle pictured below Bill Ruger's portrait was an aborted attempt to take the Mini-14 design and turn it into a big-game, semi-automatic rifle that would fire a 30-caliber cartridge. The Mini-14 only loaded a 22-caliber bullet (although the rifle would eventually also be chambered for a 30-caliber load) and thus could take smaller, varmint-style animals but not the bigger trophies, i.e., deer. The rifle, known as the XGI, was never brought into full production for one, simple reason, namely, it didn't hit the broad side of a barn. I think this had something to do with the design of the barrel but I'm not sure.

Anyway, this was the image of the company in 1985 – a company making products for hunting and shooting sports. Meanwhile, by 1985 the United States was experiencing the beginning of a crime wave that saw the violent crime rate jump from 540 per 100,000 in 1984 to more than 730 in 1990, a 35% in only five year and the largest, five-year increase in violent crime recorded since 1960, if not before. Meanwhile, notice how gun makers like Ruger responded to the crime wave from the perspective of products – they didn't.

Now take a look at the current Ruger catalog. The first page is the new Ruger tactical rifle, the SR556, immediately followed by several pages promoting the polymer, concealable gun known as the KC9. This gun is smaller than the Saturday Night Special that Uncle Ben sold in pawnshops for thirty bucks. And it is designed for one purpose and one purpose only, namely, as concealed protection from all the criminal hordes. Except there aren't any hordes. The national violent crime rate is literally half of what it was in the early 1990s. And this at a time when the proportion of Americans who own guns keeps going down. What's going on here?

Part of the answer, the most prosaic part of the answer involves the appearance of handguns from an Austrian designer named Gaston Glock, whose presence in the American gun market since the 1980s has probably been the single, most important reason for the gun industry's turn toward self-protection as the major selling-point for its products. Glock's rise to market prominence was not just due to the transition from steel to polymer frames in handgun production, but more important were the design innovations which allowed consumers to move to smaller, concealable weapons without suffering any serious loss of firepower. The full-size Glock pistol, such as the Model 17 in 9mm, has a magazine capacity of 17 rounds, but the mid-size, concealable gun, the Model 19, uses a magazine with a 15-round capacity, and the ultra-concealable 9mm pistol, the Model 26, can be loaded to a capacity of 11 rounds (10 in the magazine plus one additional round in the chamber), which is more than twice the capacity of a pocket-size, concealable revolver such as the Smith & Wesson Model 36.

I remember when *Smith & Wesson* announced with great ballyhoo that they were going to start shipping their concealable, "airweight" J-frame revolver, known as the Model 37, which had an alloy frame and weighed, unloaded, about one pound. Meanwhile, when *Glock's* Model 26, weighs five ounces more but carries twice as many rounds. And when you want to reload the Glock, just hit the magazine release button, drop out the empty mag and insert a new loaded magazine with another 10 rounds. Want to carry a 5-shot "speedloader" around for the Model 37? You'll be standing there fumbling to line up the cartridges with the cylinder holes while the other guy has reloaded his *Glock* with twice as much ammo and is ready to go.

If you're willing to forego the ballistics of a full-powered round like a 9mm or a 40, you can always drop back to the smaller and lighter Model 42, which holds 6 rounds of .380 ammunition but weighs just 13 ounces, making it what Glock says is "ideal for pocket carry." On the other hand, why sacrifice stopping-power when you can turn to the *Ruger* LC9, which holds 8 of the more-powerful 9mm cartridges and weighs only 4 ounces more than the Model 42. Ruger claims that its gun "provides slim, lightweight and compact personal protection." *Smith & Wesson* has added a laser to its concealable guns, and tells consumers that "there's a thin, red line between prepared and unprepared." But prepared for what?

Several writers have attempted to answer that question by setting out to discover the underlying cultural premises that create a demand for concealable guns. The most recent is a monograph by a Professor of Sociology at the University of Toronto named Jennifer Carlson, who journeyed a few times from Toronto down to Flint, Michigan to interview a couple of urban cowboys who like to walk around with guns. In *Citizen-Protectors: The Everyday Politics of Guns in an Age of Decline*,[1] Carlson fashions a *weltanschauung* view of the armed citizen phenomenon, arguing that CCW is a response to the alienation of rust-belt life whose victims feel abandoned by corporations that close down factories and leave towns, cops and other government agencies that refuse to respond to the needs of inner-city residents, and society in general which ignores communities that are left behind in the transition to post-industrial society. These people are on their own and start carrying guns in response to the vulnerabilities of their dead-end lives.

Carlson's book was published in 2015. Ten years earlier the same publisher, Oxford University Press, published another book explaining the gun "culture" written by another female sociologist, Abigail Kohn, who also hung out at a couple of shooting ranges, interviewed some gun guys and wrote a book called *Shooters – Myths and Realities of America's Gun Cultures.*[2] Like Carlson's book, this is also an effort to bridge the gap between two very different communities, high-brow academics on the one hand (and female academics to boot) versus low-brow gun guys who, in general, feel disquieted in the face of "feminism and civil rights;" in other words, like Carlson's narrative, guns as a response to changes that make gun owners feel vulnerable, angry and afraid.

The defense of gun ownership as a response to social-cultural change is really no different from the argument made by the NRA insofar as the organization now defines itself as America's "oldest civil-rights organization" with those "rights" being embodied in the Constitution with particular emphasis on the 2nd Amendment right. That the NRA consciously aligns itself with the conservative wing of the Republican Party is no accident, after all, current political conservatism is based on the notion that things have changed and most, if not all of those changes aren't for the good. The fact that these changes have been brought about by new culture, or economics, or racial and gender values is a nuance that need not be of concern. The bottom line is that gun ownership, particularly gun ownership for personal defense, is the gun owner's way of expressing his fear or his anger about a new world which has no room for him.

This facile and somewhat clichéd version of why gun owners are different from the "rest of us" may fit a certain preconceived set of values sustained by the educated, literate classes. But to assume that gun owners make a conscious effort to justify their guns through a serious and sustained examination of the socio-cultural forces that are arrayed against their devotion to guns is to make an assumption about a decision-making process that has no basis in truth. Or at least has never been studied to see whether it has any basis in fact.

Notwithstanding the ban on CDC-funded gun research since 1997, there have been upwards of 800 peer-reviewed studies about gun violence and related subjects published in various peer-reviewed, public health journals, and not a single study has been concerned with anything remotely connected to figuring out why people, certain people, own guns.[3] This extraordinary knowledge gap might be justified were gun ownership to be a universal event. But it is not. In fact, the percentage of Americans who own guns keeps going down to the point that even the raw number of gun owners has begun to decline. Furthermore, when a researcher like Jennifer Carlson paints a portrait of gun owners as believing that a gun can protect them from crime, this decision reflects the behavior of only a tiny percentage of Americans who have actually been the victims of violent crime. At best, less than 1% of all violent crime victims resist their attacker with a gun; most people deal with a criminal threat by yelling or running away.[4]

When Barack Obama uttered his famous "cling to guns and religion" comment he was derided by both the Left and the Right. But you know what? Effectively there's no difference between his explanation for why people own guns versus the learned, academic jargon put forward by Carlson and Kohn. We know everything that could be known about who owns guns – White men, ages 30-60, living in smaller towns in the South or in parts of the rural Midwest. But there are plenty of people who fit that profile and don't own guns. How come some do and some don't?

It has to do with the one behavioral element that binds together everyone who has a gun. It doesn't matter whether the guns are in the hands of good guys or bad; it doesn't matter if the gun is carried or stuck in a drawer at home. It doesn't matter whether it's the one gun that is owned or if it's one out of the collection of two-hundred guns. The behavior that unites all of these gun owners is one and the same and it's a behavior that we call *impulse*, what the dictionary calls "a sudden strong or unreflective urge or desire to act."

The problem with conversations between gun owners and writers like Carlson, Kohn or, for that matter, Dan Baum, is that they only talked to gun people after the impulsive act – acquiring a gun – had already taken place. So sit someone down, buy them a hamburger in a greasy spoon, tell them you're "interested" in why they carry a gun and of course your subject will become reflective, will spend a few minutes thinking things through, may even wax a little philosophical. But that's all after the fact. If you really want to know why he bought that gun is to stand behind the counter in a gun shop and watch and listen to what people say *before* they buy the gun. And know what you'll hear? You'll hear them tell you that they really don't need another gun but, what the hell, the money's in their pocket, they've figured out how to sneak it into the house past the old lady, and it's always fun to have another gun. I have sold over 14,000 retail guns and I can tell you that this is basically what everyone said. None of them needed a gun; they just wanted a gun. Or they wanted another gun.

And this unthinking, impulsive behavior not only occurs when people decide to get their hands on a gun; it also is what motivates people to carry a gun as well as to use a gun. Most of the people walking around with guns have not been the victims of crime. Why not? Because for the most part violent crime doesn't occur in neighborhoods which contain most of the legal guns. Most violent crime occurs in disadvantaged, inner-city zones; it's fact of life, like it or not, of poverty both in the United States and everywhere else. I am writing this narrative in an office located one mile away from the ghetto street corner of Springfield, MA in which 6 gun homicides have already occurred this year. One mile in the other direction from this street corner is the comfortable suburb of Longmeadow, MA. Know how many gun murders have taken place in Longmeadow over the past five years? None. How many in the past ten years? None.

Meanwhile, most of the people walking around Mason Square in Springfield, which is where all these shootings take place, are also *not carrying guns.* So why do a relatively few get up in the morning, put a gun in their pocket and hitch up their pants? We don't know. But we do know that when and if they use that gun, it's not some carefully-planned event. It's the culmination of some fuck you's back and forth, then someone pushes someone else, then out comes the gun.

And if impulse can be blamed as the determining factor in gun homicides and gun assaults, it's certainly the case for the largest category of gun violence, namely, the violence that some gun owners wreak against themselves. More than half of the 40,000 suicides committed each year in America involve the use of a gun. And suicide is almost always an unthinking, last-second, impulsive event. We certainly can't say that we know why most people who commit suicide take themselves up and through the final act because many more people express thoughts about suicide than actually pull it off. And their decision to go the last step is often clouded by pills, booze or both. So it's not the use of the gun *per se* that makes suicide so impulsive, but maybe it is. Again, we just don't know.

What we do know is that impulsive behavior is invariably involved when people decide to acquire items which they really don't need or can't explain why they have acquired same. And this is the basis, after all, for virtually all consumer marketing because rarely do consumers spend money on what we call "necessities," and even when they do, the choice of necessity is almost always based on whim, or impulse, or what appeals at that moment to the consumer as he/she decides what to buy. After all, is there really any difference between a Toyota Celica and a Honda

Accord? The name – that's it. Is there any difference between a Sig, a Ruger or a Glock? The name – that's it. But we do have an objective and reasonable need to own a car. One can't make the same argument for walking around with a gun.

Hence the existence and the strength of the armed citizen myth. Because nobody likes to believe they didn't have some reason for laying out five, six or seven hundred bucks. So they tell themselves that they want to be "safe" from crime. And this is what they hear from the gun companies all the time. And since the message is reinforced by movies, videos and everything else, the message and the myth takes on a life of its own. And every once in a great while they actually read a story about someone who faced down a bad guy with a gun or maybe there's even some talk about so-and-so in the neighborhood who protected himself with a gun. Yesterday (September 27) there was a story out of Houston where two bad guys tried to carjack a parked vehicle while the driver was asleep inside. A struggle ensued, a passerby pulled out a gun, fired a shot and the two would-be carjackers ran away. Unfortunately, the good Samaritan shot the driver of the car in the head. Do you believe that anyone who walks into a gun shop in Houston today to buy a gun to defend himself is going to change his mind because some idiot pulled out a gun to protect another citizen and shot the guy he was supposed to be protecting dead?

The whole point about the armed citizen myth is that people who believe it have long since decided, for whatever reason, that the myth can't be untrue. Which means that studies which show that guns are a risk are of no consequence or value at all. If you believe that 216 out of 318 million Americans live in states that allow just about anyone to walk around with a gun because of the "power" or the "influence" of the NRA, then you don't understand the armed citizen myth at all. The truth is that I don't understand it either. Or I should say that I don't understand why anyone believes it. But that's the whole point about myths – there's no real connection between how the myth explains something and what we really can prove to be true. And that's exactly why some people like guns.

NOTES

CHAPTER 1

1.   For gun ownership trends followed by the *General Social Survey*, see "Trends of Gun Ownership in the United States, 1972-2014," General Social Survey (March, 2015), http://www.norc.org/PDFs/GSS%20Reports/GSS_Trends%20in%20Gun%20Ownership_US_1972-2014.pdf

2.   *ibid.*

Chapter 2

1.   For a list of colonial gun-control statues, see Robert Spitzer, Guns *Across America, Reconciling Gun Rules and Rights* (New York: Oxford University Press, 2015).

2.   *ibid.*, p. 45.

3.   See the complete text of LaPierre's post-Newtown speech at: http://www.washingtonpost.com/politics/remarks-from-the-nra-press-conference-on-sandy-hook-school-shooting-delivered-on-dec-21-2012-transcript/2012/12/21/bd1841fe-4b88-11e2-a6a6-aabac85e8036_story.html

4.   *Law Center To Prevent Gun Violence* keeps a current state gun law listing: http://smartgunlaws.org/about-gun-laws/

5.   Baum and Carlson book titles. P 43.

6.   http://www.detroitarms.com/michigan-ccw-class/

Chapter 3

1.   http://www.bjs.gov/content/pub/pdf/vdhb.pdf

2.   http://sblog.s3.amazonaws.com/wp-content/uploads/2015/04/2015-03-30-NRA-Jackson-Cert-Petition-Reply-Master-FINAL.pdf.

3. Pew's millennial surveys are here: http://www.pewresearch.org/topics/millennials/

Chapter 4

1. For the NCVS methodology and survey, see http://www.bjs.gov/index.cfm?ty=dcdetail&iid=245#Methodology.

2. Kleck's study was published in a student-run law review and can be read here, among other locations: http://www.guncite.com/gcdgklec.html

3. See http://www.politico.com/magazine/story/2015/02/defensive-gun-ownership-gary-kleck-response-115082

4. Kleck has referred to Lott's study as "garbage in, garbage out." http://crimeresearch.org/2015/08/a-response-to-mother-jones-mistake-filled-effort-to-discredit-john-lott/

5. John Lott, Jr., *More Guns, Less Crime,* (Chicago: University of Chicago Press, 1998). The book is now in its 3rd edn.

6. Studies abound on the cost of gun violence beginning with work published by Philip Cook in the 1970's. The latest is: http://www.motherjones.com/politics/2015/04/true-cost-of-gun-violence-in-america

7. Solicitor Jackson's Miller brief can be read here: http://www.guncite.com/miller-brief.htm

8. Some of the pre-2008 growth of conservative legal doctrines and their attachment to the 2nd Amendment is nicely summarized in A. Winkler, Gunfight – The Right To Bear Arms in America, (New York: Norton, 2011), esp. Chapter 8.

9. Levinson's article, "The Embarrassing Second Amendment," originally appeared in the *Yale Law Journal,* 99 (1989), 637-659 and has been gleefully reprinted in endless right-

wing legal websites and pro-gun venues. A nice reprint can be found here: http://www.keepandbeararms.com/information/XcIBViewIte m.asp?ID=178

10. See: http://www.guninformation.org/freedom.html.

11. http://reclaimdemocracy.org/powell_memo_lewis/

12. All of the quotes from the *Heller* case can be found here: https://www.law.cornell.edu/supct/html/07-290.ZS.html.

Some of the more notable 2nd-Amendment scholarship can be found in, Saul Cornell & Nathan Kozuskanich, The Second Amendment on Trial, Critical Essays on District of Columbia v. Heller (Amherst, University of Massachusetts Press, 2013); and Saul Cornell, A Well Regulated Militia, The Founding Fathers and the Origins of Gun Control in America (New York, Oxford University Press, 2006); Michael Waldman, The Second Amendment, A Biography (New York: Simon & Schuster, 2014).

Chapter 5

1. It's still the best book on the Holocaust: Raul Hilberg, *The Destruction of the European Jews* (London: Holmes & Meier, 2002), 3rd edn.

2. http://www.ushmm.org/wlc/en/article.php?ModuleId=1 0005407.

3. Stephen Halbrook, *Gun Control in the Third Reich* (Oakland, Independent Institute, 2013.)

4. http://www.stephenhalbrook.com/waco.html .

5. Robert F. Williams, *Negroes With Guns* (Martino Publishing, Mansfield Centre, CT, 2013), p. 13.

6. *ibid.*, p. 113.

7. Nicholas Johnson, *Negroes and the Gun, The Black Tradition of Arms* (Amherst, NY, Prometheus Book, 2014.)

Chapter 6

1.   J. Carlson, Citizen-Protectors, The Everyday Politics of Guns in an Age of Decline (New Yotk: Oxford University Press, 2015).

2.   A. Kohn, Shooters, Myths and Realities of America's Gun Cultures (New York: Oxford   University Press, 2004).

3.   D. Hemenway & D. Webster, "Guest Editorial: Increasing Knowledge for the Prevention of   Firearm   Violence," Preventive Medicine, 79 (2015), p. 3.

4.   D. Hemenway & Sara Solnick, "The epidemiology of self-defense gun use: Evidence from the   National   Crime   Victim Surveys, 2007-2011," Preventive Medicine, 79 (2015) pp. 22-27.

ABOUT THE AUTHOR

Michael R. Weisser was born in Washington, D.C., educated in New York City public schools and received a Ph.D. in Economic History at Northwestern University. He is a featured blogger with Huffington Post and also blogs about guns at www.mikethegunguy.com. Since 1978 he has been a firearms retailer, wholesaler, law enforcement distributor and importer with total gun sales in excess of 30,000 handguns, rifles and shotguns. He is also a Life Member of the NRA and a certified firearms instructor in six specialties. He can be reached at his blog or at mike@mikethegunguy.com.

www.ingramcontent.com/pod-product-compliance
Lightning Source LLC
Chambersburg PA
CBHW030010290326
41934CB00005B/286